# Classic
# Dinners
## in one hour

**Tom Griffith**

*Penmarin Books*

*Dedicated to*

*My wife and best friend Mary,*

*who is the wind beneath my wings,*

*and to my father, who unfortunately never*

*got the chance to see this book published.*

*Editorial Offices:*
Penmarin Books
P.O. Box 286
58 Oak Grove Avenue
Woodacre, CA 94973

*Sales and Customer Service Offices:*
National Book Network
4720 A Boston Way
Lanham, MD 20706
(800) 462-6420

Penmarin Books are available at special discounts for bulk purchases for premiums, sales promotions, or education. For details, contact the Publisher. On your letterhead, include information concerning the intended use of the books and how many you wish to purchase.

**Library of Congress Cataloging-in-Publication Data**

Griffith, Thomas L.
    Classic dinners in one hour / Thomas L. Griffith.
       p.   cm.
    Includes index.
    ISBN 1-883955-05-X
    1. Dinners and dining.  2. Quick and easy cookery.  3. Menus.
    I. Title.
    TX737.G76   1995                  95-40432
    641.5'55--dc20                     CIP

Text design by Hal Lockwood
Composition by ProImage
Jacket design by GM&B Advertising
Cover photograph and interior color photographs by Jim Heric
Food styling by Kathleen Prisant

Printed in the United States of America

95 96 97 98 99 RRD 9 8 7 6 5 4 3 2 1

# Contents

sautéed onions, green peppers, and tomatoes, seasoned with oregano, rosemary, and basil. Served with mashed bean patties with red pepper flakes, and cheddar cheese corn polenta.

## Veal Dinners 87

### Veal Chops Cordon Bleu 88
Veal chops stuffed with cheese and ham, egg-dipped and breaded in seasoned bread crumbs, then oven baked. Served with sweet-and-sour red cabbage with apples and buttered spaetzel.

### Veal Chops Baked in 90
### Sour Cream and Mushrooms
Boned veal chops, sautéed and blended with onions, mushrooms, Madeira, and sour cream, then baked, and garnished with chopped pimientos. Served with pasta twists sautéed with caraway seeds and cabbage, and flavored with white wine vinegar.

### Stuffed Veal Rolls with 92
### Vegetable Sauce
Thin veal cutlets layered with ham slices and stuffed with sautéed onions, bread crumbs, and parsley, then rolled and poached in chicken stock and topped with a carrot-and-onion vegetable sauce. Served with steamed broccoli in lemon-garlic oil, and a spinach–red onion salad with bacon bits and fresh-grated Parmesan cheese.

### Veal Bourguignonne 94
### on a Bed of Pasta
Boned veal chops browned in oil and simmered in beef stock and red wine with leeks, carrots, mushrooms, garlic and sage. Served over egg noodles with corn blended with eggs, cream, and cheddar cheese, cooked until set.

### Veal Scaloppine in 96
### Mushroom Gravy on Rice
Thin veal scaloppine lightly browned and blended with sautéed onion, mushrooms, white wine, diced tomatoes, sherry, and mushroom gravy. Served over white rice with brussels sprouts poached in bouillon, vermouth, and nutmeg, with a lemon butter

### Veal Parmigiana on a Bed of Pasta 98
Veal cutlets, egg-dipped and breaded in Parmesan cheese and seasoned bread crumbs, then browned, baked in an Italian sauce, and topped with melted Swiss cheese. Served on a bed of spaghetti, with a sauté of garlic, onions, and celery.

### Breaded Veal Scaloppine 100
### with Olive Tomato Sauce
Egg-dipped veal scaloppine, sautéed until lightly browned, topped with a green olive, tomato, onion, garlic, and wine sauce, with oregano and basil. Served with sautéed mushroom caps and buttered peas.

### Veal Marsala with 102
### Fettuccine Alfredo
Veal steaks sautéed in butter with mushrooms, lemon juice, and Marsala, garnished with lemon slices and capers. Served with fettuccine blended with sour cream, cream cheese, wine, fresh-grated Parmesan cheese, and buttered peas.

## Lamb Dinners 105

### Pan-Broiled Lamb Chops with 106
### Leeks in Cream Sauce
Thick lamb chops rubbed with garlic and pan-broiled. Served with poached leeks in a thick cream sauce, blended with tarragon, basil, and thyme, and peas with fresh mint leaves and sugar.

### Mixed Lamb English Grill with 108
### Carrot Fritters
Boned lamb chops, pan-fried with sausage, bacon, chicken liver, onions, and tomatoes. Served with shredded carrots blended with eggs, flour, and milk, then fried to make fritters, and seasoned mashed potatoes with brown gravy.

### Pan-Broiled Lamb Chops 110
### Stuffed with Sausage
Lamb chops stuffed with sausage and pan-broiled. Served with vermicelli pasta blended with Swiss cheese, egg, milk, and nutmeg, then baked, and with poached endive, onions, and peas, lightly buttered.

## Garlic-Fried Lamb with Mint Sauce    112
Small lamb chops rubbed with garlic and oil, then pan fried, with a fresh mint, sugar, and wine-vinegar sauce. Served with a thick, browned-onion soup, topped with fresh Parmesan cheese and poached cabbage mixed with Swiss cheese and nutmeg, then baked.

## Lamb Fricassee in Cream Sauce    114
## on Fettuccine
Boned lamb sautéed in garlic butter, then blended with béchamel sauce and simmered with diced onions, thyme, and sage. Served over fettuccine pasta with a cassarole of layered braised lettuce, oregano, sliced tomatoes, mushrooms, and Fontina cheese.

# Brunches    117

## Crab and Asparagus with Monterey    118
## Cheese Sauce on an English Muffin
Toasted, buttered English muffin, topped with blanched asparagus spears, fresh crab meat, and a Monterey Jack cheese-cream sauce. Served with a tomato, green onion, and butter lettuce salad with a basil garlic dressing.

## Eggs Benedict with Fresh Fruit    120
Toasted English muffin with ham slice, topped with a poached egg and hollandaise sauce. Served with fresh strawberries, grapes, and melon.h strawberries, grapes, and melon wedges.

## Quiche Lorraine with    122
## Wilted Spinach Salad
A quiche with a bread crust and layers of onion, Swiss cheese, bacon, and shallots, topped with an egg-and-milk mixture, sprinkled with nutmeg, and baked. Served with a warm, wilted spinach salad, with a hint of vinegar.

## Clam Chowder with Corn Fritters    124
A rich clam chowder with potatoes, bacon, onion, celery, shallots, and basil, simmered in cream with baby clams. Served with creamed corn blended with flour, sugar, and eggs, then fried into fritters.

## Scallop, Cheddar, and Onion    126
## Omelet with Sour Cream
Whisked eggs blended with Tabasco and cream, cooked with chopped scallops, onion, and cheddar cheese, folded over and topped with sour cream and fresh chives. Served with a garlic butter sauté of portabello, oyster, and button mushrooms.

# Desserts    129

# Napkin Folding    133

# Preface

I wrote this book for those who enjoy cooking but often don't have the time, as well as for those who have limited cooking experience but would like to prepare and serve classic dinners quickly and with style.

*Classic Dinners in One Hour* offers recipes for complete meals that may be served at an intimate candlelight dinner for two or prepared for everyday enjoyment. All recipes and timetables have been developed so the meal can be completed in one hour or less, preparation and cooking time included. Unlike other cookbooks, all recipes in this book are complete meals, not just the entrees, and all recipes serve two, making them ideal for singles or for working couples. Margin notes indicate how each dinner may be expanded to serve four.

I have taken great care to write concise, step-by-step instructions for those with limited cooking experience. Once started, a recipe should be followed straight through, because the preparation is included in the timing. For example, you will see instructions to set the table or to take a break with your guests. This is all part of the total timing of the dinner. For ease of preparation, at the top of each recipe I have included the total preparation time, a list of all ingredients, and a list of utensils needed. In addition, in the recipes, professional cooking tips and techniques are printed in *italic* type, and there is an illustrated section on Classic Tips and Techniques that begins on page 7.

Every effort should be made to purchase specific brands of ingredients when named in the instructions, because extensive research has gone into developing flavors that blend well. Substitution of ingredients other than brand-name ingredients will alter the flavor of the end product. However, not all name brands may be available in your area.

For the total dining experience, in the Introduction you will find sections on table setting and wines. In the back of the book are appendixes on napkin folding and desserts that may be prepared ahead. If you are going to fold napkins, you should finish this before starting the recipe, because time to fold napkins is not included in the one-hour time frame.

All recipes in this book have been tested by nonprofessional cooks such as my students. However, if you find difficulty in understanding any recipe please write to me at 204 Albion Court, Novato, CA 94947. Please include both a day and evening phone number.

Cooking should be enjoyable and, most of all, fun. It is my hope that this book will show you just how simple and easy it can be.

## Acknowledgments

My very special thanks to all my friends— "the gang"—and to Janet for their never-ending support, and for all those pounds they gained by consuming these meals time and time again until I got them right. And my thanks to you for purchasing this book. May it bring you as much satisfaction and pleasure as it has me in developing it.

TOM GRIFFITH

# Introduction

## Setting the Table

There are a few simple rules for setting the table. First, guests should have ample elbow room; 30 inches from center of plate to center of plate is ideal if your table permits.

If you are acting as host and serving the meal, I suggest using a service plate (see the illustrations). This is a plate on which all other plates are set. The use of a service plate allows you to heat and prepare the dinner plates in the kitchen and serve without disturbing your guests once they are seated.

Utensils are basically arranged in the same order as the meal is to be eaten, starting from the outside and working toward the plate. Handles of the silver should be aligned and about 1 inch from the table edge. Set your table with only the silver to be used for the meal.

In a normal setting for a three-course dinner of salad, entrée and dessert (see illustration below), the salad fork is placed to the left of the dinner fork if the salad course is served before the entrée. If the salad is to be served after the entrée, the salad fork is placed to the right of the dinner fork.

The knives are placed with the cutting edge of the blade facing the plate. The use of a salad knife is optional but allows one to clear the salad plates without placing a used knife on the entrée service plate.

The dessert spoon or fork—whichever is to be used for dessert—is placed at the head of the plate. Water glasses are optional, but if used, they should be placed at the tip of the knives or knife. The wine glass goes slightly below and to the right of the water glass. If you are serving wine in chilled glasses, a nice

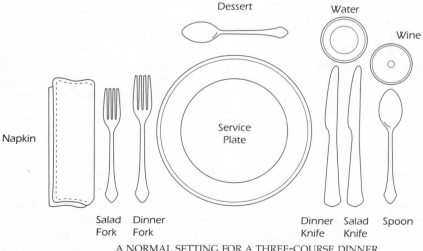

A NORMAL SETTING FOR A THREE-COURSE DINNER.

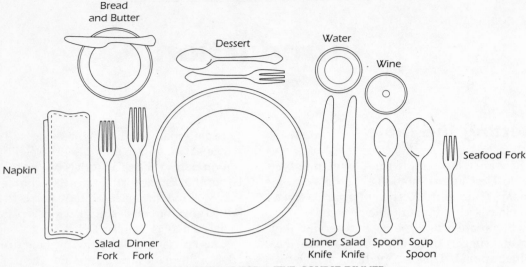

Bread
and Butter

Dessert

Water

Wine

Napkin

Salad   Dinner
Fork    Fork

Dinner Salad  Spoon  Soup
Knife  Knife         Spoon

Seafood Fork

A FORMAL SETTING FOR A FIVE-COURSE DINNER.

touch is to set the table with wine glasses but to replace them with chilled glasses as wine is served.

If salad is served with the dinner, the salad plate is placed to the left above the forks.

Napkins may be placed to the left of the forks or on the service plate, decoratively folded. In the back matter of this book you will find an appendix on napkin folding that will add an elegance touch to your table. If you attempt napkin folding, iron the napkins flat, using spray starch on both sides. This will give the cloth the rigidity needed. Napkins should be folded prior to starting to prepare dinner.

In the illustration above, you will see a formal table setting like you might find in a fine restaurant. This is appropriate for a five-course dinner, which might include a seafood appetizer, soup, salad, entrée, and dessert. The illustration indicates where silver is to be placed, but it is better to have not more than three utensils on either side of the service plate at any one time. In this case, the seafood fork and soup spoon are presented as those courses are served, and placed on the service plate.

The bread and butter plate is placed to the left of the service plate on the same level as the water glass, with the butter knife in place as shown. A butter ball or curl may be placed on each plate prior to seating guests.

If the honored guest is a woman, she is seated to the right of the host; if a man, to the left of the hostess.

When coffee is served, the cup and saucer are placed to the right of the service plate.

Service is always from the right side, removal from the left. The exception to this is when serving from a platter or serving dish. Then the platter is presented to the guest from the left.

## Wines

The world of wines and which wine goes best with what food can sometimes seem mysterious, but I will give you some basic general guidelines to help sort it out. Once you get started, you will develop your own tastes. I will not confuse you with vintages, dates, or the technical side of wine making. With some exceptions, price is a good indicator of the quality. The more expensive, the better the quality. After tasting wines for a while and keeping notes, you will develop your ability to distinguish dry white wines from sweet white wines or light-, medium-, or full-bodied red wines. It is also a good idea to ask a knowledgeable person at your wine shop for his or her opinions and recommendations.

The wines I have recommended with the menus in this book will get you started, but wine selection is largely a matter of personal taste. Although I prefer dry whites and full-bodied reds, your tastes may differ, so experiment.

Get one dry and one semi-dry or fruity white wine and do your own tasting with dinner. Do the same with a light- and a full-bodied red wine. This is fun, and you will soon learn your particular preferences in wine. Once you learn your preferences, you can taste two of the same varietal from different vintners. It won't take long until you have a list of your favorite wines, vintage dates, and vintners.

## About Red Wines

It is a misconception that red wines get better with age; some do and some do not. This mainly depends on the quality of the original grape, the amount of tannin, and other factors. Red wines contain more tannin than whites, which is why reds store or "rack" longer. The alcohol content will vary, but alcohol is practically flavorless. The alcohol content is usually printed on the bottom of the label, and the wine must fall within ± 1½ percent of its stated alcohol content.

As a general rule, reds should be aged 3 to 4 years before being consumed. All wines should be stored in a cool, dark place—ideally at 55 degrees. This is sometimes difficult to do without air conditioning, so find a closet or the coolest place you can and store wines close to the floor. Always store wines on their side with the liquid in contact with the cork. This prevents the cork from drying out and the air from seeping into the bottle, which may cause the wine to spoil.

Red wines should be served at room temperature. This does not refer to normal room temperature but to "cellar temperature," which is about 60 degrees. It won't hurt to place a red wine in the refrigerator for 30 minutes to cool it down.

Allowing a red wine to breathe means the wine is allowed to sit uncorked and undisturbed for about 20 minutes. This allows the wine to "open up" in flavor. Try this with a good, full-bodied red wine like a Cabernet Sauvignon. Uncork the wine and taste it. Now let it sit for 20 minutes and taste it again. You should notice a smoother taste.

*Estate-bottled* means the wine was produced with grapes grown on the winery's property. The vintner had total control over the growing of the grape, and the wine was produced and bottled on the winery property. This should be a superior-quality wine, depending on the producer and the wine maker.

*Vintage* means the year the grape was grown. However, if you are not a connoisseur, don't let vintage dating be a guide. Again, price will usually be an indicator of quality.

## About White Wines

White wines range from dry to sweet. The sweetness is determined by the sugar content of the grape. The wine classification chart opposite will help you distinguish dry from sweet wines and to determine which foods may go best with which wines.

Generally, white wines are consumable 2 to 4 years from the vintage date. Whites should be served chilled, about 45 to 50 degrees. The average refrigerator temperature is about 40 degrees.

# Wine Classification Chart

| Type of Wine | Recommended Varietal | Food |
| --- | --- | --- |
| **Red Wines** | | |
| Light-bodied | Gamay Beaujolais<br>Napa Gamay | Ham<br>Lamb, all preparations<br>Veal<br>Turkey<br>Cornish hens, roasted<br>Liver<br>Pâté<br>Sweetbreads<br>Cheese, Camembert,<br>  Gruyère |
| Medium-bodied | Merlot<br>Pinot Noir | Pasta with meat or cheese<br>Veal<br>Game fowl<br>Pâté, liver |
| Full-bodied | Cabernet Sauvignon<br>Zinfandel<br>Petite Syrah<br>Barbera | Beef, steaks<br>Filet mignon<br>Roasted or grilled beef<br>Duck<br>Goose<br>Game fowl |
| **White Wines** | | |
| Dry | Sauvignon Blanc<br>Fumé Blanc<br>Grey Riesling<br>Blanc de Blanc<br>Chardonnay | Oysters<br>Fish<br>Lobster<br>Fish in white sauce<br>Fowl<br>Lamb, roasted<br>Chicken in white sauce<br>Pasta with fish<br>Cheese fondues |
| Fruity, semi-dry | Chenin Blanc<br>Gewurztraminer<br>Green Hungarian<br>White Riesling<br>Johannisberg Riesling | Oysters<br>Fish<br>Fish in melted butter<br>Oily or semi-oily fish<br>Sweetbreads<br>Bouillabaisse<br>Sautéed chicken |
| Sweet | Basically, any late harvest wine will be on the sweet side, or any wine with residual sugar over 1 percent. This will be stated on the label. | All desserts<br>Fruit |

I prefer dry whites and have made recommendations in this book based on my tastes. Again, your tastes may differ, so experiment with your friends and try different wines with dinner.

## About Champagne

Champagne is not only elegant but versatile. Champagne (many domestic champagnes are called sparkling wines) generally goes with any food, and may also be drunk before and after meals. Champagnes range from dry to sweet, the driest being Brut and Extra Dry in that order; the medium-sweet champagnes being Sec and Demi-Sec, and the sweetest being Doux.

Champagnes should be consumed within 2 to 3 years of bottling—again, with some exceptions. Champagne does not have to be costly to be good. Here again, personal taste will be your best guide.

Champagne should be served well chilled—about 35 to 40 degrees. Chill champagne before opening. If not chilled, the cork may explode from the bottle, and you may get fizzing instead of the usual "pop" of the cork. You do not want to lose bubbles or effervescence. Usually, the smaller the bubbles in the glass, the better the quality of the champagne.

## Opening Champagne

The pressure behind a champagne cork is about 90 pounds per square inch, or about the same pressure as in a bus tire. When removing the wire, always keep your thumb on the cork. You may not be able to stop it from popping, but you will feel it coming out and have time to turn the bottle in a safe direction. Never aim the bottle at anyone, and be careful of your windows or the cork may end up in your yard.

To open champagne, remove the wire top. Hold the bottle so an air pocket extends from the bottle into the neck. Holding the cork firmly, twist the bottle counterclockwise. You have more control of the bottle than the cork, and that is why you twist the bottle and not the cork. When you feel the cork pushing out, hold tightly and let the pressure hiss out slowly. This way you will not lose any of the effervescence, and despite popular opinion, this is the proper and classic way of opening champagne.

Another method is to keep the bottle vertical on the counter and twist the cork out. This will give you the "pop," but the champagne will not fizz over as long as it is properly chilled. This technique is used when quantities of champagne need to be opened at the same time, as at a wedding reception.

# Classic Tips
# and Techniques

## To Peel Garlic Easily

1. Cut off root end.

2. Holding pointed tip of end of clove, strike garlic clove with the side of a heavy knife to crack skin.

3. Holding pointed tip, shake clove vigorously. Peeled clove should drop out.

## To Crush or Mince Garlic

1. Place peeled clove on cutting board. With heel of hand on side of heavy knife blade, crush clove.

2. With heel of hand applying pressure to side of knife blade, angle blade up and drag across clove.

3. Angle blade down and drag across clove. Rapidly continue this process in a rocking motion until garlic is crushed to desired texture.

## To Purée Garlic

1. Place salt on cutting board. Place clove on salt and follow the procedure for mincing garlic. The salt acts as an abrasive, like sandpaper, and will purée the garlic.

## To Dice Onion
### (Medium or large dice)

This process utilizes the entire onion with no waste.

1. Skin onion and cut off root end. Cut onion in half. Make a series of horizontal cuts the size of dice desired, but do not cut all the way through.

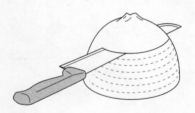

2. Make a series of vertical cuts the size of dice desired, leaving sections attached at end.

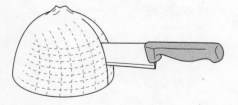

3. Slice down across cuts and onion is diced. Turn the small end piece on its side and dice to desired size.

## To Dice Onion Finely
### (Bournvise or small dice)

1. Peel onion and cut off both ends. Make a series of vertical cuts, $\frac{1}{16}$ inch or $\frac{1}{8}$ inch apart, about $\frac{3}{4}$ of the way through onion.

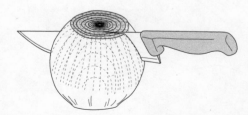

2. Rotate onion 90 degrees and make a series of vertical cuts, ¹⁄₁₆ inch or ¹⁄₈ inch apart, three-quarters of the way through onion.

3. Holding onion together, turn it on its side. Cut across cuts ¹⁄₁₆ inch or ¹⁄₈ inch apart to dice onion.
   Save unused onion for stock or soup pot.

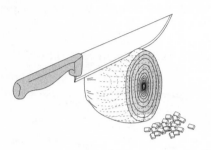

## To Seed and Dice Pepper

1. Remove stem and cut pepper in half. Remove seeds and white membrane because it tends to be bitter.

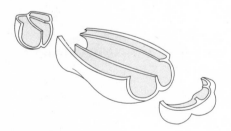

2. Cut off ends. Slice pepper into equal strips the size of dice needed.

3. Slice strips into dice size. Chop ends.

## To Julienne Carrots

Julienne strips are ¹⁄₁₆ inch x ¹⁄₁₆ inch x 2 ½ inches.

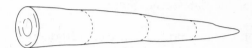

1. Peel carrot and cut off ends.
   Cut carrot into 2½-inch lengths.
   "Square" carrot sections by cutting sides to make a square.
   This will prevent carrot from slipping.
   Save waste for stock or soup pot.

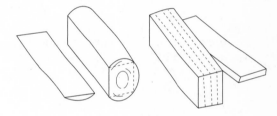

2. Make a series of vertical cuts ¹⁄₁₆ inch apart, making "boards."

3. Cut boards into ¹⁄₁₆-inch strips.

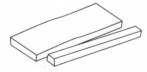

Batonnette cut is large julienne or ¼ inch x ¼ inch x 2 ½ inches.
This process can be used to julienne carrots, zucchini, or squash, and it is an easy way to large dice a potato or make French fries by using larger cuts.

## To Slice Zucchini, Carrots, or Celery

This process makes a more attractive plate presentation and yields larger slices for better plate coverage.

1. Cut off ends and slice on a 20-degree angle to desired thickness.

Make sure all cuts are the same thickness to assure even cooking of all slices.

## To Slice or Mince Fresh Leaf Herbs

*Note:* Herbs are always the fragrant leaves of fresh or dried plants like basil, mint, parsley, rosemary, oregano, tarragon, and so on. Spices are the seeds, berries, roots, bark, or fruit of various plants or trees like nutmeg, ginger, cinnamon, clove, pepper, and the like.

1. Place leaves on top of each other.

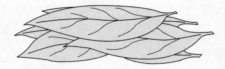

2. Tightly roll into a tube and slice in very fine strips. This is a *chiffonade* cut.

To mince, finely chop chiffonade strips.

# Chicken Dinners

Chicken Milanese with Dijon Basil Cream Sauce
on a Bed of Pasta

Broiled Chicken Breasts in Barbecue Rum Sauce

Poached Breast of Chicken with Flambéed Cognac Cream Sauce

Chicken à la Milanese with Béarnaise Sauce

Chicken Cordon Bleu in Flaky Pastry

Scottish Eggs and Herbed, Roasted Cornish Game Hens

Chicken Breasts Stuffed with Swiss Cheese Dressing
in Italian Sauce

Herb-Parmesan Baked Chicken Breasts

Chicken Parmigiana on a Bed of Pasta

Apricot Honey Chicken with Mandarin Oranges

# 🌹 Chicken Milanese with Dijon Basil Cream Sauce on a Bed of Pasta

*Skinless, boned chicken breasts with bread crumb coating, browned in butter with a Dijon mustard, cream, and basil sauce, served over egg noodles, with sautéed cabbage and stewed tomatoes. Recommended wine: Johannisberg Riesling.*

---

Once started, follow recipe through to the end without stopping.

Heat oven to 250 degrees.
Place two wine glasses in freezer to chill.

Skin and bone chicken breasts. Place chicken pieces between wax paper and pound with rolling pin or skillet to flatten and spread. Set aside. *(Chicken breasts should be the same thickness throughout to assure even cooking.)*

In a bowl, beat 2 eggs and 2 teaspoons water with fork. Set aside. With knife, shred 2 cups cabbage into ½-inch-thick slices and set aside.
Peel outer skin from green onions and cut off roots. Thin slice onions, including part of the green end, and set aside.

Place 3 quarts water in pot for pasta, salt the water, and add 1 tablespoon butter.
Place over high heat.

In sauce pan, combine ¾ cup mayonnaise, ¾ cup heavy cream, 2 tablespoons Dijon mustard, 2 teaspoons basil, and ¾ of the green onions. Place over medium-low heat.

In a skillet melt 3 tablespoons butter over medium-low heat.
Place bread crumbs in large bowl and set aside.

Set the table and take a 5-minute break with your guest.

Stir Dijon sauce and reduce heat to low.
Add 4 ounces egg noodles to boiling water and stir.

Add cabbage to butter and stir to coat all of the cabbage.
Drain stewed tomatoes. Add tomatoes to cabbage and blend. Add 2 teaspoons sugar and mix well.
In a skillet, melt 4 tablespoons of butter over medium-high heat.

## Total time: 45 minutes

## Ingredients

2½  chicken breasts
    Wax paper
2   eggs
1   small cabbage
4   green onions
    Butter
¾   cup mayonnaise
¾   cup heavy cream
2   tablespoons Dijon
    mustard
2   teaspoons basil
    Seasoned bread
    crumbs
4   ounces medium egg
    noodles
1   14½-ounce can
    stewed tomatoes
2   teaspoons sugar

## Utensils needed

Two skillets, sauce pan,
pot for pasta.

*(Do not allow butter to burn. If butter burns, clean skillet and start over. Burnt butter will permeate the flavor, and your dish will taste burnt.)*
Dip chicken in egg, then bread crumbs, coating it well on both sides.
Turn butter to medium heat and sauté chicken until browned.

While chicken sautés, place two ovenproof plates in oven to warm. *(Warmed plates will keep food hot about 30 percent longer than cold plates, allowing you time to serve without food cooling.)*

Stir Dijon sauce.
Set background music, light candles, seat guest and open the wine.
*(Don't forget the chilled glasses.)*

Turn chicken over to brown other side.

Drain pasta and rinse under very hot water. Remove plates from oven, place pasta on each plate, place chicken on side of pasta, and spoon sauce over both. Sprinkle remaining green onion over top. Add cabbage to plate and serve.

Serves two.

To serve four, add two more chicken breasts, shred 4 cups cabbage, cook 8 ounces noodles. Follow the same directions.

## ⚝ Broiled Chicken Breasts in Barbecue Rum Sauce

*Skinless, boned chicken breasts, brushed with a brown sugar, vinegar, Tabasco, Dijon mustard, and rum barbecue sauce and broiled. Served with potato slices browned in oil and sautéed onion wedges, zucchini slices, and tomatoes with basil. Recommended wine: Grey Riesling.*

---

Once started, follow recipe through to the end without stopping.

Heat oven to 350 degrees.
Place two wine glasses in freezer to chill.

Skin and bone chicken breasts and set aside.

In a bowl, combine 2 tablespoons Dijon mustard, 2 tablespoons brown sugar, 2 tablespoons vinegar, 1½ tablespoons Worcestershire, ⅛ teaspoon Tabasco, and 3 tablespoons rum. Mix until brown sugar is blended.

Brush both sides of chicken with sauce and place in baking dish.
Save remaining sauce.
Place chicken in oven.

Quarter the onion and cut one quarter in four wedges, then set aside.
Slice zucchini into ¼-inch-thick slices and set aside. *(Slice on diagonal for larger slices. See Tips and Techniques. It is important to make all slices the same thickness to assure proper cooking of all slices.)*
Cut tomato into eight wedges and set aside.

In a skillet, heat ½ cup olive oil over medium heat. Peel potato and slice into ³⁄₁₆-inch-thick slices, then set aside.

Set the table.

Brush chicken with sauce and return to oven.
Take a 5-minute break with your guest.

Increase oil to medium-high heat.
Dry potato slices with a paper towel. Add potatoes to oil and shake skillet so potatoes do not stick.

In a second skillet, melt 2 tablespoons butter over medium heat.

Brush chicken with more sauce and return to oven.

**Total time: 45 minutes**

### Ingredients

2 half chicken breasts
2 tablespoons Dijon mustard
3 tablespoons brown sugar
2 tablespoons vinegar
1½ tablespoons Worcestershire
⅛ teaspoon Tabasco
3 tablespoons rum
1 white onion
2 zucchini
1 tomato
Olive oil
1 large potato
Butter
Salt and pepper
1 teaspoon basil
2 tablespoons seasoned bread crumbs

### Utensils needed

Small baking dish, two skillets.

Add onion to butter and stir.
Turn potato slices over when lightly browned.

Set background music, light candles, seat your guest and open the wine.

Add zucchini to onions, salt and pepper to taste, and mix. Add 1 teaspoon basil and stir.

Add more sauce to top of chicken, place on top rack of oven, and turn heat to broil.

Stir zucchini.
Check potatoes and turn them to brown both sides.

Add 2 tablespoons bread crumbs to zucchini and stir.

Place two ovenproof plates on bottom rack of oven to warm. *(If plates are cold, they will draw the heat out of the food and your dinner will get cold quicker.)*

Remove potatoes from the oil and drain on paper towels or newspaper.

Add tomatoes to zucchini and stir lightly.

Remove chicken from oven. Remove plates and place chicken on each plate. Spoon any excess sauce over chicken. Add zucchini and tomatoes to the plate, then the potatoes, and serve.

Serves two.

To serve four, add two more chicken breasts. Use half an onion, two zucchinis, two tomatoes and two potatoes. Follow the same directions.

## ✿ Poached Breast of Chicken with Flambéed Cognac Cream Sauce

*Skinless, boned chicken breasts, poached in wine, and served on a bed of blanched spinach, topped with a flambéed cognac and onion cream sauce with a mushroom garnish. Served with buttered parsley potatoes. Recommended wine: Chardonnay.*

---

| Total time: 45 minutes |
|---|

### Ingredients

| | |
|---|---|
| 2 | half chicken breasts |
| | Butter |
| | Dry white cooking wine |
| 1 | bunch spinach |
| 1 | white onion |
| 4 | large mushrooms |
| 1 | potato |
| | Salt |
| ½ | cup cognac |
| 1 | cup heavy cream |
| 2 | teaspoons cornstarch or arrowroot |
| | Parsley flakes or fresh parsley, finely chopped |

### Utensils needed

Small baking dish, skillet, pot, and large pan.

---

Once started, follow recipe through to the end without stopping.

Place two wine glasses in freezer to chill. (*Serving white wine in frosted glasses adds a nice touch to the dinner ambiance.*)
Preheat oven to 350 degrees.
Set the table.

Skin and bone chicken breasts, but save the skin.
Generously butter an 8- x 10-inch baking dish.
Place chicken breasts in dish and add 1 cup white wine. Set aside.

Pinch stems off spinach leaves and rinse spinach in cold water, then discard the stems, and set spinach aside. (*Be sure spinach leaves are thoroughly washed or you will get an unpleasant gritty texture when you eat them.*)

Finely mince the onion and set aside. (*See Tips and Techniques for easy ways to mince onion.*)

Wash mushrooms, cut off stems, and discard, setting the caps aside.

Peel potato. Slice potato into ⅛-inch-thick slices. (*Be sure all slices are the same thickness so they will all cook at the same rate.*)

Fill large pan with cold water. Salt the water, add potato slices, and place over medium-high heat.

Place chicken in oven and poach 15 minutes or until just done. (*When chicken is opaque in the center of the thickest part, it is done. Check this by inserting a knife.*)

Meanwhile, place 1 quart water in pot for spinach and bring to boil over high heat. Do not add spinach.

While water is coming to boil, melt 1 tablespoon butter in skillet over medium heat.
Sauté onion and chicken skins for 5 minutes.

Add ½ cup cognac and carefully ignite at side of skillet. Shake skillet until all flame is gone.

Remove chicken skins and discard.

Add 1 cup heavy cream, ½ teaspoon salt, and ¼ cup white cooking wine. Whisk until blended and just starting to bubble. Reduce heat to low.

To serve four, add two more chicken breasts. Use two bunches spinach and two potatoes. Follow the same directions.

Set background music, light the candles, and seat your guest.

Place two ovenproof plates in oven to warm. *(Warmed plates will keep food hot 30 percent longer than cold plates will.)*

In a glass, mix 2 teaspoons cornstarch and 2 teaspoons water.

Add mixture to cream sauce and whisk until sauce thickens. *(If the sauce does not thicken quickly, increase heat and continue to cook. Sauce will thicken when just under the boiling point.)*

Place mushrooms in boiling water.

Drain potatoes and return to pan over low heat. Add 2 tablespoons butter, and stir until butter is melted and potatoes are coated. Add 1 tablespoon parsley flakes, salt and pepper to taste, and stir.

Place spinach in boiling water with mushrooms and blanch (or boil) for 45 seconds. Immediately pour into strainer and drain.

Remove plates from oven and place a bed of spinach on each plate. Top with chicken breast and spoon sauce over the chicken.

Add two mushrooms to top of chicken for garnish, add potatoes to plate, and serve.

Open the wine and enjoy. *(Don't forget the chilled glasses. Chilled, frosted glasses add a classy touch to your dinner.)*

Serves two.

## 🎀 Chicken à la Milanese with Béarnaise Sauce

*Skinless, boned chicken breasts, egg-dipped and browned in butter, served over white rice and topped with béarnaise sauce. Served with julienne carrots sautéed in sweet vermouth. Recommended wine: Chenin Blanc.*

---

**Total time: 45 minutes**

---

### Ingredients

| | |
|---|---|
| 2 | sticks butter |
| 4 | eggs |
| 1 | shallot |
| 2 | large carrots |
| 2 | half chicken breasts |
| ⅛ | cup dry cooking wine |
| ⅛ | cup tarragon vinegar |
| | Tarragon |
| | Basil |
| 1 | pouch Success Rice™ |
| 2 | tablespoons olive oil |
| 1 | cup flour |
| | Sweet vermouth |
| | Fresh parsley |

---

### Utensils needed

Two skillets, sauce pan, 2-quart pan, whisk.

---

Once started, follow recipe through to the end without stopping.

Place two wine glasses in freezer to chill.
Preheat oven to 200 degrees.

Divide one stick of butter in half, then cut each half into pats, and set aside.
Separate two egg yolks into a small bowl, and set aside.
Finely dice shallot, and set aside.

Peel carrots. To julienne, cut lengthwise in ⅛-inch-thick strips. Cut these strips into ⅛-inch-thick sticks. Cut sticks into 3-inch lengths, and set aside. *(To cut carrots evenly, "square" the carrot by cutting each side flat. This will prevent the carrot from rolling and will make cutting much easier. See Tips and Techniques.)*

Skin and bone chicken breasts, and set aside.

In a sauce pan, combine ⅛ cup cooking wine, ⅛ cup tarragon vinegar, 2 teaspoons tarragon, 1 teaspoon basil, and diced shallots. Place over medium heat, and stir and cook until liquid is almost gone (about 8–10 minutes). *(Reducing the mixture increases and concentrates the flavor. If a liquid is reduced by 50 percent, it will be 50 percent stronger in flavor.)*

While the tarragon mixture cooks, beat two eggs in a bowl with a fork, and set aside.

Place 6 cups water in pan for rice, salt the water, and place pan over high heat.

Add 2 tablespoons butter to one skillet and melt over low heat. Take a short break with your guest while butter melts.

When tarragon mixture is reduced, remove from heat, add the two egg yolks, and whisk until mixture is light and frothy.

Return to heat and add half of the butter pats. Whisk until butter is melted and sauce is smooth. Add remaining butter pats and whisk until sauce smooths. Remove from heat.

Add 2 tablespoons butter and 2 tablespoons olive oil to second skillet and place over medium heat.
Add 1 pouch Success Rice™ to boiling water.

Place 1 cup flour on paper towel and dredge chicken breasts in flour. Set aside.

Set the table, set background music, light the candles.

Add carrots to skillet with butter.
Add 2 tablespoons vermouth to carrots and turn heat to medium. Stir often.

When butter is melted in second skillet, dip chicken in beaten egg and place in butter oil.
Cook about 6 minutes, turning frequently.

While chicken cooks, place two ovenproof plates in oven to warm. (*Warming plates will keep food hot 30 percent longer because the plate will not extract heat from the food.*)

Seat your guest and open and serve the wine. (*Don't forget chilled glasses.*)

Return béarnaise sauce to low heat and whisk.*

Drain rice and place it on a warm plate. Top rice with chicken breast and spoon béarnaise sauce over the chicken. Add carrots, garnish with fresh parsley, and serve.

Serves two.

To serve four, add two more chicken breasts, julienne three carrots, and use two pouches rice. Follow the same directions.

* If béarnaise sauce separates, it's because it got too hot. Drop one ice cube into sauce and whisk briskly until sauce comes together. Serve immediately.

## (§) Chicken Cordon Bleu in Flaky Pastry

*Skinless, boned chicken breasts, poached in wine, then topped with ham and Swiss cheese, wrapped in pastry, egg washed and baked to a golden brown. Served with sautéed zucchini strips and a tomato-onion salad with a red wine vinegar, mustard, and curry dressing. Recommended wine: Grey Riesling.*

| Total time: 55 minutes |
|---|

### Ingredients

2   half chicken breasts
    Butter
    White cooking wine
2   zucchini
    Olive oil
1   tablespoon red wine vinegar
½   teaspoon dried mustard
    Pinch of curry powder
1   head butter lettuce
1   large tomato
1   red onion
1   package prebuttered filo dough, 4 inches wide *
2   ham slices ⅛-inch thick
    Sliced Swiss cheese
1   egg

### Utensils needed

Small baking dish, skillet, baking sheet.

Once started, follow recipe through to the end without stopping.

Place two wine glasses and two salad forks in freezer to chill.
Preheat oven to 350 degrees.
Set the table.

Skin and bone chicken breasts, and remove white tendon from underside. Generously butter baking dish. Form chicken breasts into small balls by folding edges under. Place chicken in baking dish and add cooking wine to a depth of ¼ inch. Place in oven and bake 15 minutes, basting frequently.

Meanwhile, slice zucchini in half lengthwise and scrape out seeds. Cut off ends and slice zucchini into ¼-inch-wide strips. Set aside.

In a bowl, combine ¼ cup olive oil, 1 tablespoon wine vinegar, ½ teaspoon dried mustard, and a pinch of curry powder. Mix well and refrigerate.
On salad plates, place a full leaf of butter lettuce. Thin slice the tomato. Slice several thin slices of onion and break them apart. Arrange tomato slices on the lettuce and the onion rings on the tomato and refrigerate.

Melt 2 tablespoons butter in skillet, add zucchini, remove from heat, and set aside.

Check chicken when just done and remove from oven. (*Chicken will have additional cooking time when wrapped in pastry. Do not overcook chicken at this stage or it will become dry.*)

Remove filo dough from refrigerator and peel off eight sheets.

*\*Note:* be sure the filo is pre-buttered, because if it is not, filo will dry out and crack, and it will not bake properly. If you cannot find 4-inch-wide filo but have pre-buttered sheet filo, cut filo into 8-inch-wide strips and use four strips instead of eight. Make cross with two strips and follow instructions from Figure 2 on.

Moisten edge of one sheet of filo with a little water. Overlap second sheet ½ inch on moistened edge (moisture will seal filo together). Repeat to form a cross (see Figure 1).

Cut ham slice into a 4-inch circle and place in center of filo cross. Place chicken breast on ham.
Tear sliced Swiss cheese into small pieces and place on chicken breast (see Figure 2).

Fold ends of filo over chicken. Fold loose end over top and roll (see Figure 3). Fold sides as you would wrap a package, and fold ends under (see Figure 4). Place on baking sheet.

Repeat process for second Cordon Bleu.

Beat 1 egg in bowl and brush top and sides of filo. Place in oven and bake *(about 20 minutes or until golden brown)*.

Take a 12-minute break with your guest.

About 8 minutes before Cordon Bleu is ready, place zucchini over medium heat and sauté, turning frequently.

A few minutes before Cordon Bleu is ready, place two ovenproof plates in oven to warm.

Remove wine glasses from freezer. Seat your guest and serve the wine.

Place Cordon Bleu on plates, arrange the zucchini, and serve.

After main course, spoon salad dressing over salad and serve salad with frozen fork. *(Serving salad after the main course comes from European countries. This way the vinegar dressing will not taint the palate for the wine, and it is a very refreshing way to conclude a meal.)*

Serves two.

To serve four, double all ingredients and follow the same directions.

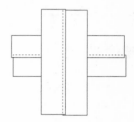

**FIGURE 1**

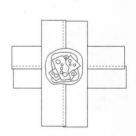

**FIGURE 2**

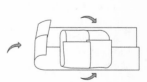

**FIGURE 3**

**FIGURE 4**

# ✿ Scottish Eggs and Herbed, Roasted Cornish Game Hens

*Golden brown, pan-roasted Cornish game hens smothered with herb butter. Served with spaetzel\* with fresh Parmesan cheese and steamed cauliflower and broccoli, and an appetizer of hard-cooked egg wrapped in sausage, breaded, and fried. Recommended wine: Grey Riesling.*

---

| Total time: 60 minutes |
| --- |

## Ingredients

3  eggs
   Butter
2  Cornish game hens (thawed)
1  cauliflower
1  bunch broccoli
2  teaspoons tarragon
2  teaspoons basil
1  teaspoon thyme
   Pepper
   Cooking oil
1  cup seasoned bread crumbs
   Small amount of flour
   12-ounce package Jimmy Dean™ sausage
1  box spaetzel
   Fresh Parmesan cheese
   Fresh parsley

## Utensils needed

Baking dish, skillet, three pans, vegetable steamer.

---

Once started, follow recipe through to the end without stopping.

Preheat oven to 350 degrees.
Place two wine glasses in freezer to chill.

Place one egg in pan of water and turn to high heat. When water comes to a full boil, remove from heat and let egg stand in water. While egg boils, melt ¾ stick butter in small pan over medium-low heat.

Wash game hens in cold water, and remove packet of gizzards. Pat hens dry and salt the cavity.
Butter baking dish, place hens in baking dish, and set aside.

Cut flowerets from half of the cauliflower and broccoli.
Prepare vegetable steamer with water, and place cauliflower and broccoli in steamer. Cover, but do not turn on heat.

Finely grate ½ cup Parmesan cheese and set aside.

To melted butter add 2 teaspoons tarragon, 2 teaspoons basil, 1 teaspoon thyme, and 1 teaspoon pepper. Stir to mix.
Spoon half the melted butter over Cornish hens, making sure to coat hens with the herbs in the butter.
Place hens in oven.

Place 1 quart water in pan for spaetzel. Do not turn on heat.
Place ¼ inch of oil in skillet and turn to medium heat.

In a small bowl, beat two eggs with a fork, and set aside.
Pour 1 cup bread crumbs onto paper towel, and set aside.

When egg has sat in hot water for 15 minutes, remove and run under cold water. Peel egg.

Roll egg in flour. *(This will prevent the egg from slipping when wrapped in sausage.)*

---

\*Spaetzel are tiny Swiss-style dumplings, usually found in the gourmet section of your local market.

Cut a 3½-inch section of sausage and pat it into a circle. Place egg in the center of sausage and mold sausage around egg, forming a ball of sausage with egg in the center.
Dip sausage ball in egg and roll in bread crumbs, coating all sides. Repeat egg dip and bread crumb coating.

Turn water for spaetzel to high. Do not add spaetzel.

Place sausage ball in hot oil and roll back and forth to cook on all sides. Stand on end to cook ends. Cook at least 12 minutes. *(To check, insert knife in sausage and spread apart. There should be no red color.)*

While sausage cooks, set the table, set background music, and light the candles. Seat your guest and serve the wine.

Spoon the remaining herb butter over Cornish hens, coating them with herbs. Return to oven.

Drain sausage on a paper towel.
Cut sausage ball in half lengthwise, place each half on small plate so egg shows, and garnish with parsley.

Add half box of spaetzel to boiling water and stir.
Turn cauliflower/broccoli to medium-high heat.

Serve Scottish egg appetizer and enjoy the first course.

When appetizer is finished, remove spaetzel from heat, cover, and let stand.
Turn cauliflower/broccoli to low heat.

Place two ovenproof plates in oven to warm, and take a 5-minute break with your guest.

Drain spaetzel in colander, return to pan, and add 2 tablespoons butter. Stir until butter is melted.
Add grated Parmesan cheese and stir. Salt and pepper to taste and return to low heat.

Remove plates from oven and place Cornish hen on each plate. Add cauliflower/broccoli, spoon spaetzel onto plates, and serve.

Serves two.

To serve four, prepare two Scottish eggs, and use all the cauliflower and broccoli. When hens are cooked, split to make four servings. Follow the same directions.

# Chicken Breasts Stuffed with Swiss Cheese Dressing in Italian Sauce

*Skinless, boned chicken breasts pounded flat, stuffed with a Swiss cheese dressing, rolled and lightly browned in butter, then baked in Italian sauce. Served with green peppers and mushrooms sautéed with thyme, and hot marinated artichoke hearts topped with fresh melted Parmesan cheese. Recommended wine: Chardonnay.*

---

**Total time: 50 minutes**

### Ingredients

2  half chicken breasts
   Wax paper
¼  cup grated Swiss cheese
1  egg
2  tablespoons seasoned bread crumbs
   Salt and pepper
   Pinch of nutmeg
   Toothpicks
   Butter
8  mushrooms
1  jar thick spaghetti sauce
1  bell pepper
1  jar marinated artichoke hearts
¼  teaspoon thyme
¼  cup fresh grated Parmesan cheese

### Utensils needed

Two skillets, small baking dish.

---

Once started, follow recipe through to the end without stopping.

Heat oven to 350 degrees.
Place two wine glasses in freezer to chill.

Skin and bone chicken breasts. Place breasts between wax paper and pound with rolling pin or heavy skillet to thin and flatten. Set aside. *(Chicken breasts should be the same thickness overall. This will allow easier rolling and ensure proper cooking.)*

Finely grate ¼ cup Swiss cheese. In a bowl combine one egg, Swiss cheese, 2 tablespoons bread crumbs, ⅛ teaspoon salt, ⅛ teaspoon pepper, and a pinch of nutmeg.
Place half the mixture in the center of one chicken breast and roll up. Secure with toothpick. Repeat with second breast.

In a skillet, melt 2 tablespoons butter over medium heat.

Cut stems from mushrooms and discard. Slice caps into thick slices, and set aside.

Set the table.

Sauté chicken rolls in butter until opaque on the outside and slightly browned. Remove chicken to small baking dish. Save skillet; do not clean. Pour 1½ cups spaghetti sauce over center of chicken and place in oven.

Cut bell pepper in half and remove seeds. Slice half of the bell pepper into ¼-inch-thick slices, cut slices in half, and set aside.
Take a 15-minute break with your guest.

In the skillet that the chicken was browned in, melt 1 tablespoon butter over medium heat. Add bell pepper to butter and stir.
In a second skillet, heat 2 tablespoons marinated artichoke oil over medium-low heat. Add artichoke hearts.

Place two ovenproof plates in oven to warm. *(Warmed plates keep the food hot for a longer time. Cold plates extract the heat from the food.)*

Add mushrooms to bell peppers and stir.
Add ¼ teaspoon thyme, salt and pepper to taste, and stir.

Set background music, seat your guest, and open the wine. *(Don't forget the chilled glasses. A frosted glass adds to the atmosphere of the dinner.)*

Finely grate ¼ cup Parmesan cheese.
Stir artichoke hearts. Sprinkle Parmesan cheese over artichokes.
Do not stir.

Stir bell peppers.
Remove plates from oven. Place chicken on each plate and spoon excess sauce over top. Add pepper-mushroom sauté, add artichoke hearts, and serve.

Serves two.

To serve four, add two more chicken breasts and double the Swiss cheese dressing. Use all of the green pepper and two jars artichoke hearts. Follow the same directions.

# ⚘ Herb-Parmesan Baked Chicken Breasts

*Skinless, boned chicken breasts, dipped in butter and breaded with Parmesan cheese, bread crumbs, and Italian herbs. Served with steamed cauliflower with a cheddar cheese sauce and a creamy sherry-spinach soup. Recommended wine: Chenin Blanc.*

---

| **Total time: 55 minutes** |

### Ingredients

- 1 cauliflower
- 1 cup grated cheddar cheese (½ block)
- 2 sticks butter
- 1 tablespoon flour
- 1 cup milk
- 2 half chicken breasts
- 1 cup Parmesan cheese
- 1 cup seasoned bread crumbs
- 2 teaspoons Italian herbs
- 1 teaspoon oregano
- 1 teaspoon sage
- 1 package Stouffer's™ frozen creamed spinach
- 1 cup cream
- 1 tablespoon sherry
- Fresh parsley

### Utensils needed

Baking sheet, three sauce pans, vegetable steamer.

Once started, follow recipe through to the end without stopping.

Preheat oven to 350 degrees.
Place two wine glasses in freezer to chill. Set the table.

Cut flowerets from cauliflower.
Prepare vegetable steamer with water and place cauliflower in steamer.
Cover, but do not turn on heat.

Grate 1 cup cheddar cheese and set aside.

In a pan, melt 1 tablespoon butter over medium heat. Add 1 tablespoon flour and whisk into butter. Add 1 cup milk a little at a time and whisk until mixture thickens. Remove from heat and set aside.

Skin and bone chicken breasts.

Melt ½ stick butter in pan.

In a bowl, combine 1 cup Parmesan cheese, 1 cup bread crumbs, 2 teaspoons Italian herb seasoning, 1 teaspoon oregano, and 1 teaspoon sage. Mix well.

Fill a third pan with water, place over high heat, and immerse pouch of frozen spinach.

Dip chicken in melted butter, coating both sides.
Drop into Parmesan–bread crumb mixture and coat well on all sides. Place chicken on baking sheet and set aside.

Return white sauce to low heat, add cheddar cheese, and blend. Take a short break with your guest.

When creamed spinach is hot, light the candles, set background music, and seat your guest.

Drain spinach, open pouch, and pour into same pan. Place over medium heat and add 1 cup cream and 1 tablespoon sherry. Stir to blend and heat until warm.

Put chicken in oven.
Turn cauliflower to high heat.

When soup is hot, serve. Pour wine (glasses in freezer) and enjoy your first course.

Approximately 15 minutes later, clear soup dishes. Put two oven-proof plates in oven to warm. *(Warming the plates keeps the food hot 30 percent longer.)*

Turn off cauliflower.
Stir cheese sauce.

When plates are warm, place cauliflower on plates, adding a pat of butter and spooning cheese sauce over top. Add chicken, garnish with parsley, and serve.

Serves two.

To serve four, add two more half chicken breasts, use two pouches creamed spinach, and add 2 cups cream and 2 tablespoons sherry. Follow the same directions.

# 🌸 Chicken Parmigiana on a Bed of Pasta

*Skinless, boned chicken breasts, wine-poached, topped with Swiss cheese, and served on a bed of spaghetti topped with Italian sauce. Served with individual garlic bread loaves and steamed sugar peas. Recommended wine: Sauvignon Blanc.*

| |
|---|
| **Total time: 40 minutes** |

## Ingredients

1  tablespoon cooking oil

2  half chicken breasts
   White wine for cooking
   Butter

2  French rolls

2  teaspoons garlic powder
   Sugar peas (fresh), enough for two

1  can Contadina™ pizza sauce

5  ounces thin spaghetti

1  package sliced Swiss cheese

## Utensils needed

Large sauce pan, pot, vegetable steamer, two small pans, small baking dish.

Once started, follow recipe through to the end without stopping.

Place two wine glasses in freezer to chill.
Preheat oven to 325 degrees.

Place 3 quarts water in pot for spaghetti, and add 1 tablespoon cooking oil, but do not turn on heat.

Skin and bone chicken breasts. Remove white tendon from underside. Butter baking dish, place breasts flat in baking dish, and add cooking wine to a depth of ¼ inch. Set aside.

Melt ¾ stick of butter in small pan.
Slice French rolls almost through, ½ inch apart. Rolls should look like a small loaf of bread.
Add 2 teaspoons garlic powder to butter, mix well, and spoon butter between slices of bread, coating both sides. Wrap in foil and set aside.

Break off end of sugar peas and pull fiber string from back. Wash in cold water. Prepare vegetable steamer with water, place sugar peas in steamer and cover, but do not turn on heat.

Place pizza sauce in small pan and turn heat to simmer.

Turn spaghetti water to high.

Place chicken in oven and baste from time to time with cooking liquid.

Set the table and the background music.

When spaghetti water boils, add spaghetti.
Turn sugar peas to high.
Place bread in oven.
Baste chicken.

Take a short break with your guest.

Just before spaghetti is ready, place two ovenproof plates in oven to warm. *(Warmed plates will keep the food hot for a longer time. Cold plates extract the heat from the food.)*

Place two layers of Swiss cheese on top of each chicken breast, and return to oven.

Drain spaghetti and rinse under very hot water.

Remove plates from oven.
Place half of the spaghetti on each plate, top with chicken breast, and spoon pizza sauce over top. Arrange sugar peas on plates and serve. Serve garlic loaves on separate small plate for each person.

Serve wine (glasses in freezer) and enjoy.

Serves two.

To serve four, add two more chicken breasts, two more French rolls, and enough sugar peas to serve four. Cook 8 ounces of spaghetti and follow the same directions.

# Apricot Honey Chicken with Mandarin Oranges

*Skinless, boned chicken breasts, sautéed with paprika, and baked in a honey, clove, brandy sauce topped with apricot preserves and Mandarin orange sections. Served with brown rice cooked in chicken stock with peas, onions, and sliced mushrooms. Recommended wine: Johannisberg Riesling.*

---

**Total time: 45 minutes**

---

## Ingredients

2 cups chicken stock (canned)
2 half chicken breasts
1 onion
6 mushrooms
1 cup long-grain wild rice (or any rice that cooks in 25 minutes)
Butter
1 tablespoon olive oil
3 tablespoons flour
1 teaspoon paprika
1 cup apricot preserves
½ cup honey
⅛ teaspoon ground clove
1 tablespoon brandy
1 tablespoon orange Curaçao or orange-flavored liqueur
1 can Mandarin oranges
1 10-ounce package frozen peas

## Utensils needed

Skillet, pot, small baking dish.

---

Once started, follow recipe through to the end without stopping.

Place 2 cups chicken stock in pot over high heat.
Place two wine glasses in freezer to chill.
Preheat oven to 350 degrees.

Skin and bone chicken breasts, and set aside.

Chop ½ onion and set aside. *(To chop onion quickly, place flat side on counter, make a series of horizontal cuts, not cutting all the way through. Next, make a series of vertical cuts the thickness of the dice needed. Now cut down across the cuts in the thickness of dice needed. See Tips and Techniques.)*

Slice mushroom caps and set aside.

Place 1 cup brown rice in boiling chicken stock, cover, and reduce heat to simmer.
Butter baking dish.

Place 1 tablespoon olive oil in skillet over medium heat.
Mix 3 tablespoons flour and 1 teaspoon paprika in zip-lock bag. Place chicken breasts in bag and shake to coat well. When oil is hot, brown the chicken breasts on both sides, about 4 minutes on each side. *(Be sure oil is hot. The chicken should sizzle when placed in oil. If oil is not hot enough, the chicken will soak up the oil instead of being seared on the outside.)*

While chicken browns, in a bowl mix together 1 cup apricot preserves, ½ cup honey, ⅛ teaspoon clove, 1 tablespoon brandy, and 1 tablespoon orange Curaçao.

When chicken is browned, place chicken in baking dish. Pour apricot mixture over chicken. Drain Mandarin oranges and add orange sections to chicken. Place in oven.

Set the table.

Add ½ package frozen peas to rice, stir, cover, and continue to cook.

Take a 15-minute break with your guest.

Add onions and mushrooms to rice and stir. Cover and continue cooking.

Place two ovenproof plates in oven to warm. *(Warmed plates prevent the heat from the food going into the plate, and your dinner will stay hot much longer.)*

Take a 5-minute break with your guest.

Remove chicken from oven.
Stir the rice.
Place rice on plates, add chicken breast, and spoon sauce and orange sections over chicken.
Open wine and serve.

Serves two.

To serve four, add two more chicken breasts. Use 2 cups apricot preserves, 1 cup honey, ¼ teaspoon clove, 2 tablespoons brandy, and 2 tablespoons Curaçao in sauce. Follow the same directions.

# Seafood Dinners

Shrimp-, Mushroom-, and Scallop-Filled Crepes
with Madeira Cream Sauce

Poached Filet of Sole on a Bed of Rice
with White Wine Cream Sauce

Clam Linguini with Garlic French Bread

Crab-and-Scallop Newburg in Puff Pastry

Catfish Fry with Potato-and-Egg Pie

Swordfish Stroganoff on Pasta

Wine-Poached Salmon with Béarnaise Sauce

Sautéed Dill Calamari Steak Strips

Sautéed Oysters with Fontina Cheese

Scampi Sautéed in Garlic Butter and Flambéed in Cognac

Red Snapper with Browned Butter and Capers

Almond-Battered Fried Halibut with Mint Potatoes

Shrimp Newburg Flambéed in Brandy

Sautéed Swordfish with Hot Cucumber Pepper Relish

# Fish Texture and Cooking Guide

| Fish | Texture | Broiled | Baked | Steamed or Poached | Sautéed or Pan-Fried | BBQ |
|------|---------|---------|-------|--------------------|----------------------|-----|
| Albacore | Soft, becomes firm with cooking | 1 | 2 | | 1 | 3 |
| Bluefish | Soft, tender | 2 | 1 | | 3 | |
| Butterfish | Soft, melting flesh | 2 | 3 | | 1 | |
| Carp | Firm | 2 | 1 | | 3 | 2 |
| Catfish | Tender | 3 | 2 | 2 | 1 | 3 |
| Cod | Tender-firm | 1 | 2 | 3 | | |
| Croaker | Tender | 2 | 3 | | | 1 |
| Flounder | Tender-flaky | 3 | 2 | 2 | | 1 |
| Grouper | Tender-firm | | 1 | 2 | | 2 |
| Haddock | Tender-chewy | 1 | 2 | 3 | | 2 |
| Halibut | Tender-firm | 1 | 2 | 3 | | 1 |
| Orange Roughy | Tender-firm | 1 | 2 | 2 | | 1 |
| Perch | Tender-flaky | 2 | 3 | | | 1 |
| Pompano | Firm | 1 | 3 | | 2 | 2 |
| Rockfish | Firm | 2 | 3 | 2 | 1 | 2 |
| Salmon | Firm | 2 | 1 | | 3 | 1 |
| Sea Bass | Tender | 1 | 2 | 2 | 3 | |
| Shark | Firm | 2 | 1 | 3 | 2 | 1 |
| Red Snapper | Tender-firm | 2 | 1 | 3 | 2 | |
| Sole | Tender-flaky | 3 | 1 | 2 | 1 | |
| Striped Bass | Tender-firm | 2 | 3 | 1 | 2 | 1 |
| Swordfish | Firm | 1 | 2 | 3 | | 1 |
| Trout | Firm | 2 | 3 | | 1 | 2 |

1 = Excellent      2 = Good      3 = Fair

# 🦀 Shrimp-, Mushroom-, and Scallop-Filled Crepes with Madeira Cream Sauce

Fresh-rolled beer-batter crepes, filled with shrimp, scallops, mushrooms, and onions simmered in a Madeira cream sauce. Served with a classic Caesar salad and steamed asparagus. Recommended wine: Grey Riesling.

---

**Total time: 60 minutes**

### Ingredients

- 3 eggs
- ¾ cup milk
- ⅔ cup beer
- Salt
- Olive oil
- 1 cup flour
- ½ pound shrimp
- ½ pound scallops
- 1 onion
- ¼ pound mushrooms
- Asparagus
- Garlic
- Croutons
- 6 anchovies
- Romaine lettuce
- 2 tablespoons lemon juice
- ½ teaspoons sugar
- ¼ cup fresh grated Parmesan cheese
- 2 tablespoons butter
- ⅔ cup sour cream
- ½ cup whipping cream
- 3 ounces cream cheese
- 3 tablespoons Madeira
- 1 tablespoon cornstarch
- Fresh dill or parsley

---

Once started, follow recipe through to the end without stopping.

Preheat oven to 250 degrees.
Place two wine glasses, two salad plates, and two salad forks in freezer to chill.
Set the table.

Crepe batter: In bowl, whisk or beat 2 eggs, ¾ cup milk, ⅔ cup beer, ¼ teaspoon salt, 2 tablespoons olive oil, and 1 cup flour until smooth. Set aside to thicken.

Peel and wash shrimp, chop them coarse, and set aside.
Chop scallops coarse, and set aside.
Finely dice ½ cup onion, and set aside.
Wash and coarse chop mushrooms, and set aside.

Prepare vegetable steamer with water. Cut asparagus tips into 6-inch lengths, and discard bottom end. Place tips in steamer and cover. Do not turn on heat.

Fill small pan with 3 inches of water and place over medium-high heat. Do not allow water to boil.

Mince 1 teaspoon garlic. (*An easy way to peel a garlic clove is to slightly crush it with the side of a knife blade. The skin will peel off easily. To mince garlic, crush clove with side of knife blade and, with pressure on the blade, move knife back and forth in a rocking motion. See Tips and Techniques.*)

In a small skillet, heat 1 tablespoon olive oil over medium heat. Add 1 cup of croutons and chopped garlic. Toss to coat croutons in garlic.

Chop six anchovies, and set aside.
Remove croutons from heat.

Teflon-coated skillet, two regular skillets, small pan, vegetable steamer.

Place 1 egg in water and cook for 2 minutes. Do not allow water to boil. Remove egg and run under cold water.

Tear enough Romaine lettuce for two salads into a bowl. Break coddled egg over Romaine and toss to coat lettuce. Add ¼ teaspoon pepper, 3 tablespoons olive oil, 2 tablespoons lemon juice, ½ teaspoon sugar, croutons, anchovies, and ¼ cup finely grated Parmesan cheese. Toss salad to coat all lettuce thoroughly and chill in refrigerator.

Melt 2 tablespoons butter in a regular skillet over medium heat. Add ⅔ cup sour cream, ½ cup whipping cream, cream cheese (broken into chunks), chopped onion, shrimp, and scallops. Stir to blend and melt cream cheese.

Brush an 8-to-10-inch Teflon skillet with oil and place over medium heat. *(Skillet is hot when a drop of water "dances" when dropped into skillet.)* Pour 2 ounces crepe batter in circle in center of skillet and quickly roll skillet to spread crepe batter over bottom, covering the entire skillet. *(¼ cup equals 2 ounces, or use a shot glass to measure crepe batter.)* Cook a few minutes, until edges start to brown.

Reduce shrimp mixture to medium-low and stir well.
Turn crepe over and cook a few seconds longer until lightly browned. Slide crepe onto plate and repeat process three more times to make four crepes.

Add mushrooms and 3 tablespoons Madeira to shrimp, and blend.

Turn asparagus to medium-high heat.

Seat your guest, set background music, and light the candles.

Place two ovenproof plates in oven to warm.
Open the wine and serve it in chilled glasses.
Place salad on frozen plates and serve with frozen forks.

When salad course is finished, turn off the asparagus.

Mix 1 tablespoon cornstarch with 2 tablespoons water. Add to shrimp mixture and stir until mixture thickens. *(If mixture does not thicken quickly, it was not quite hot enough. Increase heat to medium and bring to just under boil.)*

Place crepe on each plate, spoon shrimp mixture across center, fold edge of crepe over shrimp mixture, and roll half a turn. Repeat with second crepe on each plate.

Spoon additional shrimp mixture over top of crepes, and garnish with fresh dill or parsley. Add asparagus to plate and serve.

Serves two.

To serve four, make eight crepes. You should already have enough batter. Use ¾ pound shrimp and ¾ pound scallops. For sauce, use 1 cup sour cream, ⅔ cup cream, 5 ounces cream cheese, and 5 tablespoons Madeira. Follow the same directions.

## ✿ Poached Filet of Sole on a Bed of Rice with White Wine Cream Sauce

*Tender filet of sole poached in white wine, served on a bed of white rice, topped with a mushroom, onion, and wine cream sauce, and garnished with lemon and chives. Served with steamed sugar peas. Recommended wine: Pinot Chardonnay.*

---

| Total time: 45 minutes |
| --- |

### Ingredients

1   small white onion
5   mushrooms
   Butter
¾   pound filet of sole
   White cooking wine
   Sugar peas, enough for two
2   tablespoons flour
1   cup Half & Half™
   Salt and pepper
1   lemon, cut in half
1   pouch Success™ rice
   Fresh parsley
   Chives (fresh or freeze-dried)

### Utensils needed

Vegetable steamer, small baking dish, three pans.

---

Once started, follow recipe through to the end without stopping.

Preheat oven to 350 degrees.
Place two wine glasses in freezer to chill.

Finely dice onion, and set aside. *(Fine dice is ⅛-inch dice. Cut skinned onion in half. Make a series of horizontal cuts ⅛ inch apart, not cutting all the way through. Next, make a series of vertical cuts ⅛ inch apart. Make ⅛-inch slices down across cuts and the onion is diced. See Tips and Techniques.)*

Wash mushrooms, cut off stems, and discard. Thin slice caps, and set aside.

Generously butter baking dish. Wash filets in cold water and place in baking dish. Add enough cooking wine to just cover filets. Set aside.

Prepare vegetable steamer with water. Wash sugar peas, break off ends, and pull "string" fiber from back. Place sugar peas in steamer and cover, but do not turn on heat.

Place 1 quart water in a pan for the rice, but do not turn on heat. Add 1 teaspoon salt.

In a small pan, melt 1½ tablespoons butter over medium heat. Watch carefully. Do not allow butter to burn,. *(If butter burns, clean the skillet and start over. Burnt butter will give the dish a burnt taste that will not cook out.)* Gradually whisk in 2 tablespoons flour to make a roux. *(A roux is a paste mixture of flour and butter used to thicken sauces and gravies. If you don't have a whisk, rapid stirring with a spoon will also work.)*

Turn rice water to high heat. Do not add rice.
Place filets in oven to poach.

To the roux gradually add ½ cup Half & Half™, whisking constantly until mixture thickens. Gradually add remaining ½ cup Half & Half™ and whisk until mixture thickens and smooths out. *(If mixture will not smooth, continue cooking, whisking constantly.)* Add 1 teaspoon salt, 2 teaspoons pepper, 2 teaspoons lemon juice from ½ lemon, ⅓ cup cooking wine, diced onion, and sliced mushrooms. Whisk to blend. Reduce heat to low, and stir occasionally.

When rice water boils, add 1 pouch Success™ rice.
Thin slice other half of lemon for a garnish. Wash and snip parsley for a garnish.

Turn sugar peas to high heat.

Set the table.
Stir the white sauce.

Take a 5-minute break with your guest.

Place two ovenproof plates in oven to warm.
Set background music, light the candles, and seat your guest.
Serve the dinner wine. *(Don't forget the chilled glasses in freezer.)*

Turn sugar peas to low heat.

Drain rice. Cut pouch open and make a bed of rice on each plate. Place poached filet on rice, top with white sauce, sprinkle chives over top, and garnish with lemon slices and parsley. Arrange sugar peas on plate and serve.

Serves two.

To serve four, use 1¼ pounds of filet of sole, enough sugar peas to serve four, and two pouches of rice. Follow the same directions. You should have enough sauce to serve four.

# 🦐 Clam Linguini with Garlic French Bread

A simmered blend of onions, mushrooms, garlic, clams, sour cream, cream cheese, and oregano, served over linguini noodles. Served with steamed broccoli flowerets and garlic French bread. Recommended wine: Chenin Blanc.

---

**Total time: 45 minutes**

---

## Ingredients

French bread
Butter
1 bunch broccoli
3 cloves garlic
1 tablespoon cooking oil
1 onion
8 ounces sour cream
1 8-ounce Philadelphia™ cream cheese
1 pint heavy whipping cream
2 6½-ounce cans minced clams
1 teaspoon oregano
1 teaspoon salt
8 ounces linguini or thin spaghetti

## Utensils needed

Sauce pan with cover, vegetable steamer, 5-quart pot, skillet.

---

Once started, follow recipe through to the end without stopping.

Place two wine glasses in freezer to chill.
Slice and butter French bread, then set aside.
Preheat oven to 350 degrees.

Prepare vegetable steamer with water. Cut flowerets from broccoli and place it in steamer. Cover, but do not turn on heat.

In a large skillet, melt ¼ stick butter over medium heat. Peel 3 cloves of garlic, crush with side of knife, and sauté in butter about 5 minutes. Do not allow butter or garlic to burn. *(If butter burns, clean the skillet and start over. Burnt butter or garlic will give the dish a harsh burnt taste that will not cook out.)*

Place 3 quarts water in pot over high heat. Add 1 tablespoon oil and salt.

Medium dice ½ onion and add to garlic. *(Medium dice is ¼-inch pieces. Cut onion in half. Lay flat side of onion on counter and make a series of horizontal cuts ¼ inch apart, not cutting all the way through. Next, make a series of vertical cuts ¼ inch apart. Slice down across cuts ¼ inch apart and the onion is diced. See Tips and Techniques.)*

Add 8 ounces sour cream, 8 ounces cream cheese broken into chunks, ½ pint whipping cream, 1 can clams (drained), 1 can clams with juice, 1 teaspoon oregano, and 1 teaspoon salt. Stir to mix. Stir occasionally to blend and melt cheese.

Place French bread in oven.
Turn broccoli to high heat.
Set the table.

Add linguini to boiling water and boil about 10 minutes, or until done.

Take a short break with your guest.

When linguini is just about done, place two ovenproof plates in oven to warm. *(Warmed plates keep food hot 30 percent longer than room-temperature plates.)*

Set background music and seat your guest.

Drain linguini when done, and rinse under very hot tap water. Return linguini to pot. Pour ¾ of the clam mixture into linguini and mix well. Place linguini on plates and spoon remaining sauce over top. Add broccoli to plate. Place French bread in basket and serve. Open wine. *(Don't forget the chilled glasses.)*

Serves two.

To serve four, cook 12 ounces linguini, dice a whole onion, and use 12 ounces sour cream, 11 ounces cream cheese, three cans of clams, and ⅔ cup cream. Follow the same directions.

## 🦀 Crab-and-Scallop Newburg in Puff Pastry

*Fresh crab and scallops, blended with cognac, sherry, diced shallots, and mushrooms, simmered in a cream sauce, and served in a golden-brown puff pastry shell. Served with wild rice cooked in chicken stock and buttered thyme peas. Recommended wine: Chardonnay.*

---

| Total time: 55 minutes |
| --- |

### Ingredients

- 2 cups chicken stock, canned
- 1 shallot
- 4 eggs
- 10 mushrooms
- 1 cup scallops
- 1 package puff pastry shells, thawed
- Butter
- 1 cup wild rice (or any rice that cooks in 25 minutes)
- 1 package frozen peas
- 1 cup cream
- ¼ cup dry sherry
- 1 tablespoon cognac
- 1 cup fresh crab meat (or cooked shrimp if crab not in season)
- 1 teaspoon thyme
- 1 tablespoon cornstarch

### Utensils needed

One pot with cover, two pans (one with cover), one skillet.

Once started, follow recipe through to the end without stopping.

Preheat oven to 400 degrees.
Place two wine glasses in freezer to chill.

Place 2 cups chicken stock in pot and place over high heat.

Set the table.

Finely chop shallot, and set aside.
Separate three egg yolks, and set aside.
Thick slice mushrooms, and set aside.
If scallops are large, cut in half, and set aside.

Beat one egg in small bowl. Remove two thawed pastry shells from package, place on baking sheet and brush with beaten egg. Place in oven.

Add 1 cup rice to chicken stock, cover, and reduce heat to low.

Melt ¼ cup butter in pan over medium heat.

Fill second pan with ¼ cup water and place over high heat for peas.

Add chopped shallot to melted butter and sauté until translucent. In a bowl, whisk 1 cup cream, ¼ cup sherry and three egg yolks. Add mixture to shallots and stir until mixture thickens slightly. Add 1 tablespoon cognac, mix, and remove from heat.

Place peas in boiling water, and cover to cook.

In a skillet, melt 1 tablespoon butter over medium heat. Add mushrooms and scallops, and sauté until mushrooms start to give up water.

Place two ovenproof plates in oven to warm.

Add crab to scallops and stir. Add sauce to mixture and blend well.

Remove peas from heat and add 1 tablespoon butter, 1 teaspoon thyme, salt and pepper to taste, and mix until butter is melted.

Mix 1 tablespoon cornstarch with 1 tablespoon water and add to crab and scallops. Stir until mixture thickens.

Remove pastry shells from oven. Cut around center and push center section down. Place bed of rice on plate. Place pastry shell on rice, fill with crab-scallop mixture, and spoon sauce over sides. Add peas to plate and serve.

Open wine and enjoy.

Serves two.

To serve four, bake four pastry shells, separate four egg yolks, and use 1½ cups cream, 1½ cups scallops, 1½ cups crab meat, and ⅓ cup sherry. Follow the same directions.

# 🦀 Catfish Fry with Potato-and-Egg Pie

Catfish filets marinated in lemon juice, garlic, and oregano, egg-dipped and breaded with corn meal, and pan-fried. Served with potato cubes layered with an onion béchamel sauce and sliced hard-cooked eggs, then baked, and a tomato, endive, and herb salad with oil and vinegar dressing. Recommended wine: Gewurztraminer.

---

**Total time: 60 minutes**

### Ingredients

| | |
|---|---|
| 6 | eggs |
| | Fresh parsley |
| 1 | small white onion |
| 1 | tablespoon chives |
| 2 | medium potatoes |
| 1 | tomato |
| 1 | head endive |
| 1 | tablespoon basil |
| | Salt and pepper |
| | Olive oil |
| 1 | tablespoon vinegar |
| | Butter |
| 2 | to 4 catfish filets, depending on size |
| ¼ | cup lemon juice |
| 1 | clove garlic |
| ½ | teaspoon oregano |
| 3 | tablespoons flour |
| ½ | teaspoon vanilla extract |
| ¼ | cup cream |
| 1 | teaspoon nutmeg |
| 1 | cup corn meal |

### Utensils needed

Pot, pan, large skillet, small baking dish.

---

Once started, follow recipe through to the end without stopping.

Place 2 quarts hot tap water in pot over high heat.
Fill pan with hot water and place over high heat. Salt water and add five eggs to hardboil.
Preheat oven to 375 degrees.
Place two wine glasses in freezer to chill.

Chop 4 tablespoons parsley, and set aside.
Fine dice onion, and set aside. *(Fine dice is ⅛-inch squares See Tips and Techniques.)*
Chop 1 tablespoon chives, and set aside.
Peel potatoes and chop into ½-inch squares. *(To chop potato easily, "square" it first. See Tips and Techniques. Make sure all potato squares are the same size to ensure even cooking.)*

Add potatoes to boiling water.

Meanwhile, cut an X in the bottom of a tomato and place it in boiling water with potatoes for one minute. *(This process is called blanching and will make the tomato skin peel easily.)*
Remove tomato and peel off skin. Slice tomato into thin slices.

Arrange endive leaves on two salad plates. Place tomato slices on endive.
In a bowl, mix 1 tablespoon parsley, 1 tablespoon chives, 1 tablespoon basil and a pinch of salt and pepper. Sprinkle herbs over tomatoes. Whisk 3 tablespoons olive oil with 1 tablespoon vinegar. Drizzle over salad and place salads in refrigerator.

In pan over medium heat, melt 3 tablespoons butter.

Rinse catfish filets in cold water. In a bowl, combine ¼ cup lemon juice, 1 teaspoon salt, 1 clove minced garlic, and ½ teaspoon oregano. Place filets in bowl, coating all sides, and chill in refrigerator.

To melted butter whisk in 3 tablespoons flour and cook 1 minute. Whisk in 1¼ cups milk a little at a time, stirring until white sauce thickens and smooths. Add ½ teaspoon vanilla extract, whisk until sauce thickens, and remove from heat.

Check potatoes *(when point of knife is inserted into potato, you should feel no resistance).*
Drain potatoes and return to pan. Set aside.

Remove eggs from heat, and drain them. Cover eggs with cold water, and set aside.

To potatoes add 2 tablespoons butter in small pieces, ¼ cup cream, and 1 teaspoon nutmeg. Mix well.
Salt and pepper to taste, add diced onion, and mix well.

Peel hard-boiled eggs and slice as thin as you can.
Butter a small baking dish and alternate a layer of potatoes, sliced egg, and white sauce. Sprinkle with parsley. Repeat, ending with a layer of potatoes on top. Place in oven.

Set the table.

In a large skillet over high heat, melt half a stick of butter. Do not allow butter to burn.
In a small bowl, beat one egg.
In a second bowl, place 1 cup corn meal.
Remove fish filets from marinade and pat dry with paper towels.
Dip filets in egg and roll in corn meal, coating both sides evenly, and set aside.

Place two ovenproof plates in oven to warm.

Wait until butter in skillet just starts to foam and place filets in skillet. Fry filets about 3 minutes until lightly browned, turn, and brown other side.

Place filets on warm plates, add potato egg pie, garnish with fresh parsley, and serve with salad. Open wine and serve.

Serves two.

To serve four, peel and slice two tomatoes and use two heads endive. Double ingredients in salad dressing, and use four to eight catfish filets. You should already have enough potato-and-egg pie to serve four.

# Swordfish Stroganoff on Pasta

Swordfish strips sautéed in butter and blended with a mushroom, onion, sour cream, wine, and cream cheese sauce. Served over green spinach egg noodles with a sauté of sliced red and yellow peppers, and garlic bread. Recommended wine: Grey Riesling.

---

**Total time: 50 minutes**

## Ingredients

| | |
|---|---|
| 1 | white onion |
| ½ | pound mushrooms |
| 2 | swordfish steaks (about 1 pound total) |
| 1 | red pepper |
| 1 | yellow pepper |
| 2 | cloves garlic |
| | Butter |
| | Salt and pepper |
| ½ | teaspoon basil |
| ½ | teaspoon oregano |
| 1 | small French roll |
| 1 | package green noodles (10 ounces) |
| 1 | cup sour cream |
| ⅛ | cup dry white wine |
| 1 | teaspoon lime juice |
| 1 | tablespoon Dijon mustard |
| 8 | ounces cream cheese |

## Utensils needed

Two skillets, pot, pans.

---

Once started, follow recipe through to the end without stopping.

Preheat oven to 270 degrees.
Place two wine glasses in freezer to chill.
Set the table.

Dice onion and set aside.
Thick slice mushroom caps and set aside.
Remove skin from swordfish and slice meat into strips ½ inch thick, then set aside.
Slice peppers in half, core, and remove seeds. Slice into ¾-inch-wide strips, then slice strips in half to make ¾- x 2-inch pieces. Set aside.

Mince garlic, and set aside. (*A quick way to mince garlic is to crush garlic with side of knife blade by applying pressure to knife blade with palm, then mince. See Tips and Techniques.*)

Place 3 quarts hot salted water in pot for noodles and place over high heat.

In a small pan, melt half a stick of butter over medium heat. Add 3 cloves minced garlic, ⅛ teaspoon pepper, ½ teaspoon basil, and ½ teaspoon oregano.

In a skillet, melt 1 tablespoon butter over medium-high heat.

Slice French roll in half lengthwise.

Mix garlic butter well. Spoon garlic butter on both halves of French roll, coating it with herbs. Place bread on baking sheet or foil and set aside.

Add onion to skillet and sauté until onion is soft. Add mushrooms and cook, stirring, until mushrooms are just starting to turn color. Meanwhile, in a bowl, whisk together 1 cup sour cream, ⅛ cup wine, 1 teaspoon lemon juice, 1 tablespoon mustard, a pinch of salt, and pepper.

Remove mushrooms and onions to a bowl and set aside.

In the same skillet, over medium heat, add 1 tablespoon butter and melt. Add fish strips and cook, turning frequently, until fish is white.

While fish cooks, in a second skillet, melt 2 tablespoons butter over medium-high heat.
Add pepper slices and sauté.

Add half a package of noodles to boiling water.
Place French roll in oven.

Cut cream cheese in chunks and add to fish. Stir to melt cream cheese. Add mushrooms and onions, stirring to mix. Cook until mixture is hot.
Add sour cream mixture, reduce heat to low, and blend until hot but not boiling.
Remove from heat.

Place two ovenproof plates in oven to warm.
Stir peppers.
Seat your guests.

Cut warm garlic bread into slices.
Drain noodles and rinse under hot water. Place noodles on plate and top with swordfish and sauce. Add sautéed peppers. Add garlic bread and serve.
Open wine and enjoy.

Serves two.

To serve four, use four swordfish steaks and 10 ounces of noodles. For sauce, use 1½ cups sour cream, ¼ cup wine, 1½ teaspoons lemon juice, and 11 ounces cream cheese. Follow the same directions.

## ⚜ Wine-Poached Salmon with Béarnaise Sauce

*Salmon steaks, poached in wine and onions, topped with a made-from-scratch Béarnaise sauce. Served on a bed of white rice with a sauté of cubed cantaloupe and tomato slices seasoned with oregano. Recommended wine: Green Hungarian.*

---

| Total time: 55 minutes |
|---|

**Ingredients**

1 onion
2 salmon steaks about
   1 inch thick
   White cooking wine
3 bay leaves
2 cups chicken stock
   (canned)
1 cantaloupe
1 large tomato
1 cup white rice
2 eggs
1 shallot
⅛ cup tarragon
   vinegar
2 teaspoons tarragon
1 teaspoon basil
1 teaspoon oregano

**Utensils needed**

Small pan, medium pan with lid, baking dish, skillet.

Once started, follow recipe through to the end without stopping.

Preheat oven to 350 degrees.
Place two wine glasses in freezer to chill.

Set the table.

Butter baking dish for salmon steaks.
Slice half the onion into ⅛-inch-thick slices. Place in baking dish.
Rinse salmon steaks under cold water. Lightly salt and pepper and place in baking dish.
Add cooking wine until three-quarters of the way up the side of salmon.
Add bay leaves and set aside.

Place 2 cups chicken stock in pan with lid. Do not turn on heat.

Divide 1 stick of butter in half, cut each half into pats, and set aside.

Cut cantaloupe in half and remove seeds.
Slice one-half into ½-inch-thick slices. Cut off rind and slice into 1-inch cubes, then set aside.
Slice tomato into ¼-inch-thick slices. Cut slices in half, and set aside.

Turn chicken stock to high heat and cover.

Place salmon in oven.
Take a 5-minute break with your guest.

Add 1 cup white rice to boiling chicken stock, stir, and cover. Reduce heat to low.

Separate two egg yolks, and set aside.
Dice shallot, and set aside.

In a small pan, combine ⅛ cup cooking wine, ⅛ cup tarragon vinegar, 2 teaspoons tarragon, 1 teaspoon basil, and diced shallot. Place over medium heat, stir, and cook until liquid is almost gone, about 8 to 10 minutes. *(Reducing mixture increases and concentrates the flavor. If a liquid is reduced by 50 percent, it will be 50 percent stronger in flavor.)*

In a skillet, melt 1 tablespoon butter over medium heat.

Stir rice, cover, and continue to cook.
Take a 5-minute break with your guest.

Add cantaloupe cubes to melted butter.

When tarragon mixture is reduced, remove it from heat and whisk in two egg yolks. *(Keep egg yolks moving until incorporated. You don't want the egg yolks to cook and set.)* Whisk until mixture is light and frothy. Return to heat and add half of the butter pats. Whisk until butter is melted and sauce is smooth. Add remaining butter pats and whisk until sauce is smooth. Remove from heat and let sit. *(If béarnaise sauce separates, it got too hot. Drop one ice cube into sauce and whisk over medium heat until sauce comes together. Serve immediately.)*

Place two ovenproof plates in oven to warm.
Stir cantaloupe. Add tomato slices and 1 teaspoon oregano.
Take a 5-minute break with your guest.

Remove cantaloupe and tomatoes from heat.
Stir rice and remove from heat.

Place rice on heated plates. Add salmon steak, top with a few onions and spoon béarnaise sauce over top. Add cantaloupe and tomatoes and serve with wine. *(Don't forget the chilled glasses.)*

Serves two.

To serve four, use two tomatoes, four more slices of cantaloupe, and four salmon steaks. Follow the same directions.

## ❧ Sautéed Dill Calamari Steak Strips

*Strips of calamari steaks breaded in flour, dill, and taco seasoning, then sautéed in garlic butter and blended with creamed spinach. Served over egg noodles. Recommended wine: Johannisberg Riesling.*

---

| **Total time: 45 minutes** |

### Ingredients

1  package frozen cream of spinach
1  onion
6  mushrooms
3  cloves garlic
2  calamari steaks
1  cup flour
1  tablespoon dill
1  teaspoon taco seasoning
   Salt and pepper
2  tablespoons butter
8  ounces egg noodles
½  cup Half & Half™
½  cup Madeira

### Utensils needed

Pot, pan, skillet.

Heat oven to 250 degrees.
Place two wine glasses in freezer to chill.
Set the table.

Fill pan with water, place over medium-high heat and add 1 package frozen cream spinach.
Fill pot with water, then salt it and place over medium-high heat.

Slice half the onion, cut slices into quarters, and set aside.
Remove stems from mushrooms, slice caps ¼ inch thick, and set aside.
Peel 3 cloves garlic, crush with side of knife, and chop fine. Set aside.

Slice calamari steaks into ¼-inch-thick slices, approximately 3 inches long.
In a zip-lock bag, place 1 cup flour, 1 tablespoon dill, 1 teaspoon taco seasoning, ¼ teaspoon pepper, and ¼ teaspoon salt. Seal and toss to mix.
Dry the calamari on paper towel, add calamari to bag, and shake to coat calamari on all sides. Let stand.

Turn water in pot to high heat.

In a skillet, melt 2 tablespoons butter over medium heat.
Take a 5-minute break with your guest while butter heats.

Add garlic, and sauté until garlic bubbles. Add onion, and sauté until onions start to become limp.
Shake excess flour off calamari, add calamari to skillet, and stir to coat calamari with butter.

Add 8 ounces noodles to boiling water in pot.

Stir calamari.
Drain cream spinach, open pouch, and add to calamari. Add ½ cup Half & Half™ and stir to incorporate. Mixture will thicken.

Add mushrooms and ½ cup white wine, stirring to blend. *(If mixture is too thick, add more wine and mix until mixture reaches desired thickness.)*

Place two ovenproof plates in oven to warm. *(Warming plates will keep food hot 30 percent longer.)*

Check noodles. When noodles are done, drain and rinse in very hot water. Place noodles on plate and spoon calamari over top. Open wine and serve.

Serves two.

To serve four, use four calamari steaks and two packages creamed spinach. Cook 10 ounces egg noodles, and follow the same directions.

# Sautéed Oysters with Fontina Cheese

Oysters, dipped in egg and coated with seasoned bread crumbs, then sautéed in butter and topped with Fontina cheese. Served with a cracked wheat pilaf, cooked in chicken stock with sautéed onions, mushrooms, celery, and pimientos. Recommended wine: Gewurztraminer.

---

**Total time: 45 minutes**

### Ingredients

- 2 eggs
- 2 cups seasoned bread crumbs
- 12 large shucked oysters
- 1 onion
- 2 stalks celery
- 1 tablespoon pimientos
- 10 mushrooms
  Fontina cheese
  Butter
- 1 cup Ala wheat bulgar
- ¼ teaspoon dill
- ¼ teaspoon oregano
  Salt and pepper
- 2 cups chicken stock
- 3 tablespoons olive oil

### Utensils needed

One large skillet and one medium skillet with covers, large pan.

---

Heat oven to 250 degrees.
Place two wine glasses in freezer to chill.

In a bowl, beat two eggs with 4 tablespoons water.
Place 1 cup seasoned bread crumbs in second bowl.
Drain oysters and dry with paper towels. Insert fork in muscle of oyster and dip once in egg and bread crumbs, and again in egg and bread crumbs, coating all sides. Coat six oysters. Add 1 cup bread crumbs and continue with remaining oysters. Place oysters on baking sheet and let sit.

Cut onion into medium dice, and set aside. (*Medium dice is ¼-inch cubes. See Tips and Techniques for quick and easy ways to dice onion.*)
Chop celery, and set aside.
Chop pimientos, and set aside.
Slice mushrooms, and set aside.
Finely grate ¾ cup Fontina cheese, and set aside.

In a medium skillet, melt 2 tablespoons butter over medium heat. Sauté onion, celery, mushrooms, and 1 cup bulgar wheat. Stir, cooking until vegetables are tender and bulgar wheat is golden. Add ¼ teaspoon dill, ¼ teaspoon oregano, ½ teaspoon salt, and ¼ teaspoon pepper, and mix well. Add 2 cups chicken stock, cover, and bring to a boil over high heat.

Set the table while pilaf comes to a boil.
When pilaf boils, stir, and reduce heat to low. Cover and let simmer.

Take a 5-minute break with your guest.

In a large skillet, melt 2 tablespoons butter with 3 tablespoons olive oil over medium-high heat. Do not allow to burn.
(*If butter burns, clean skillet and start again. Burnt butter will give the oysters a burnt taste.*)
Place two ovenproof plates in oven to warm.

When butter and oil are hot, add breaded oysters to skillet. Sauté a few minutes and turn over. Sauté until browned. Place six oysters on each plate and sprinkle grated Fontina on top.
Add pilaf to plate, open the wine, and serve.

Serves two.

To serve four, use 24 oysters and grate 1½ cups Fontina cheese. You should already have enough wheat pilaf. Follow the same directions.

# 🦐 Scampi Sautéed in Garlic Butter and Flambéed in Cognac

Fresh scampi sautéed in garlic butter and flambéed in cognac with a sauce of white wine, sherry, onion, mushroom, Dijon mustard, and diced tomato. Served over rice, with sautéed cucumber and yellow squash slices. Recommended wine: Blanc de Blanc.

---

**Total time: 50 minutes**

### Ingredients

| | |
|---|---|
| 18 | scampi or medium prawns |
| 2 | cups chicken stock |
| 2 | cloves garlic |
| | Fresh parsley |
| 1 | large tomato |
| 1 | red onion |
| 1 | cup long-grain and wild rice or any rice that cooks in 25 minutes |
| 8 | mushrooms |
| 1 | cucumber |
| 2 | yellow crookneck squash |
| | Butter |
| 2 | ounces cognac |
| 1 | tablespoon Dijon mustard |
| | Lea & Perrins White Wine Worcestershire™ |
| 2 | ounces sherry or Madeira |
| ½ | cup white wine |
| 1½ | teaspoons cornstarch |

### Utensils needed

Pan with cover, large skillet, medium skillet.

---

Once started, follow recipe through to the end without stopping.

Preheat oven to 250 degrees.
Set the table.

Peel scampi and set aside.
In a pan, place 2 cups chicken stock over high heat for rice.

Peel and chop garlic, then set aside. (*An easy way to peel garlic is to cut off the root end and, holding the point of skin, lightly crush clove with side of knife blade to break skin. Garlic clove should shake out of skin. See Tips and Techniques.*)
Chop 2 tablespoons parsley, then set aside.
Cut tomato in half and squeeze out seeds. Chop tomato and set aside.
Slice three slices of red onion, then cut slices in half, and set aside.

Add 1 cup rice to boiling water, stir, reduce heat to low, and cover.

Wash mushrooms, cut off stems and discard. Slice caps, and set aside.
Slice cucumber and yellow squash into ¼-inch-thick slices. Set aside. (*See Tips and Techniques for slicing on diagonal. Make sure all slices are the same thickness. This will allow proper cooking of all slices.*)

In a medium skillet, melt 2 tablespoons butter over medium heat. Do not allow butter to burn. (*If butter burns, clean skillet and start over. Burnt butter will cause the dinner to have a burnt taste.*)

In a large skillet, melt half a stick of butter over medium heat.

Take a 5-minute break with your guest.

Add cucumbers and squash to butter in medium skillet, and mix to coat.
Add garlic to large skillet and sauté a few minutes.

Place two ovenproof plates in oven to warm.

Add scampi to large skillet, toss and sauté 2 minutes, turning until scampi are pink. Pour 2 ounces cognac into skillet and carefully ignite at side with match. Stir until all flame is gone. Remove scampi to plate, but save skillet and cooking liquid. Place scampi in oven.

Stir squash, and salt and pepper it to taste.

Place scampi skillet over medium heat, and add sliced mushrooms, 1 tablespoon Dijon mustard, 1 teaspoon white wine Worcestershire, onion slices, 2 ounces sherry or Madeira, and ½ cup white wine. Mix to blend.

Mix 1½ teaspoons cornstarch with 1 teaspoon water. When mushroom mixture is just at boil, stir in cornstarch to thicken.

Add chopped tomatoes. Cook 2 or 3 minutes to heat tomatoes.

Remove plates from oven. Place bed of rice on each plate. Spoon mushroom sauce over rice, top with scampi, and sprinkle with chopped parsley. Add cucumber squash sauté. Open wine and serve.

Serves two.

To serve four, use 24 to 30 prawns, 2 large tomatoes, 16 mushrooms, 2 cucumbers, and 4 squash. Follow the same directions, adding 1 cup wine to sauce.

# 🦐 Red Snapper with Browned Butter and Capers

*Red snapper filets covered with browned butter, shallots, parsley, capers, and lemon, then baked. Served with spinach wilted in garlic butter and sprinkled with Pernod, and sliced, buttered baked potatoes topped with grated cheddar cheese. Recommended wine: Sauvignon Blanc.*

| |
|---|
| **Total time: 60 minutes** |

### Ingredients

4   tablespoons
   unsalted butter
2   white potatoes
   Olive oil
   Dried chives
1   bunch spinach
2   cloves garlic
1   shallot
2   tablespoons minced
   parsley
1   tablespoon capers
1   lemon
2   snapper filets
   (¾ pound total)
   Salt and pepper
4   ounces cheddar
   cheese
1   teaspoon Pernod
   (licorice-flavored
   liqueur)

### Utensils needed

Skillet, small pan, baking dish, baking pan.

Once started, follow recipe through to the end without stopping.

Preheat oven to 375 degrees.
Place two wine glasses in freezer to chill.

Melt 2 tablespoons butter over medium heat.

Rinse potatoes and dry with paper towel. Rub potatoes with olive oil and cut into thin slices—but not all the way through—to form a fan. Drizzle with melted butter, salt to taste, and sprinkle with chives. Place potatoes in baking pan, and set aside.

Remove stems from spinach, wash leaves, drain, and set aside.
Mince garlic, and set aside.
Dice shallot, and set aside.
Mince 2 tablespoons parsley, and set aside.
Blot 1 tablespoon capers on paper towel. Mince capers, and set aside.
Finely grate 1 teaspoon lemon rind (yellow part only), and set aside.
Squeeze 2 teaspoons lemon juice from lemon, and set aside. *(Before cutting lemon, apply pressure to lemon with palm and roll on counter. This will break up the flesh and make juicing easier.)*

Place potatoes in oven.

Melt 2 tablespoons butter in small pan over medium-high heat until it just starts to brown.
While butter melts, butter a 6- x 10-inch baking dish.

Stir shallots into melted butter and cook until shallots are soft. Remove from heat and stir in 2 teaspoons fresh lemon juice.

In a bowl, combine parsley, capers, and lemon rind zest.

Place snapper filets in baking dish, skin side down. Salt and pepper filets to taste. Brush filets with browned butter. Sprinkle with parsley-caper mixture, and set aside.

Set the table.

Place filets in oven with potatoes.
Grate cheddar cheese, and set aside.

In a skillet, melt 2 tablespoons butter over medium-high heat with minced garlic. When butter is melted, add spinach leaves and cook, turning constantly until slightly wilted. Drain off moisture. Salt and pepper to taste, and sprinkle with 1 teaspoon Pernod.
Mix well. Remove from heat.

Place two ovenproof plates in oven to warm.

Remove potatoes from oven. Sprinkle top with grated cheddar cheese and return to oven.
Remove filets and plates from oven.
Turn oven to 500 degrees to brown potatoes.

Seat your guest and open the wine.

Place filet on plate, and add spinach. Remove potatoes from oven and add to plate.
Serve with wine in chilled glasses.

Serves two.

To serve four, double all ingredients and follow the same directions.

# ⚸ **Almond-Battered Fried Halibut with Mint Potatoes**

Halibut filets marinated in lemon juice, battered with ground almonds, egg, almond extract, and bread crumbs, then sautéed in oil. Served with diced potatoes with fresh mint butter, and a spinach, corn, and diced tomato sauté. Recommended wine: Grey Riesling.

---

| |
|---|
| **Total time: 55 minutes** |

## Ingredients

2 halibut or sole filets, about ¾ pound total
½ cup lemon juice
  Fresh mint
  Butter
1 bunch spinach
2 Italian or Roma tomatoes
1 can whole-kernel corn
2 potatoes
½ cup fresh-grated Parmesan
  Olive oil
2 ounces slivered almonds
2 eggs
1 teaspoon almond extract
⅔ cup milk
2 tablespoons bread crumbs
1 tablespoon cornstarch
½ cup flour
  Tabasco

## Utensils needed

Skillet with cover, skillet, medium pan, small pan.

Once started, follow recipe through to the end without stopping.

Place two wine glasses in freezer to chill.
Preheat oven to 250 degrees.
Place filets in bowl, pour ½ cup lemon juice over top, and let marinate.

Finely chop 15 mint leaves and place in small pan. (*To chop mint leaves easily, stack leaves on top of each other. Tightly roll the leaves and thinly slice the roll with knife. This is called a* chiffonade *cut. See Tips and Techniques.*)
Add 4 tablespoons butter, and set aside.

Wash spinach and remove stems. (*Spinach is grown in sandy soil, so be sure to wash leaves well or they will have a gritty texture when eaten.*)
Dice tomatoes into ½-inch squares, and set aside.
Drain corn, and set aside.
In a skillet with lid, melt 2 tablespoons butter over medium heat. Do not cover at this time.

Peel potatoes and dice into 1-inch pieces. Place in medium pan, and fill with water to cover potatoes by 1 inch. Salt the water, and place over medium heat.

Set the table.

Add spinach to melted butter, and mix to coat. Cook until spinach starts to wilt.

While spinach cooks, grate ½ cup Parmesan cheese, and set aside.
Stir spinach and take a 5-minute break with your guest.

Add corn to spinach, cover, and continue to cook.

In a second skillet, add just enough oil to lightly coat bottom of skillet: 1 to 1½ tablespoons. Place over medium-high heat.

In a food processor or coffee grinder, finely grind almonds.
In a bowl, beat 2 eggs, 1 teaspoon almond extract, and ⅔ cup milk.

Whisk in 2 tablespoons bread crumbs, ground almonds, and 1 table-spoon cornstarch. Set aside.

Place mint butter over medium heat to melt. Do not allow to burn.

Place two ovenproof plates in oven to warm.

Pat filets dry with paper towels. Place ½ cup flour in bowl and lightly dredge filets in flour, shaking off excess. Coat filets in almond batter. Place in hot oil and reduce heat to medium.

Remove mint butter from heat.

Add diced tomatoes to spinach, salt and pepper to taste, and add four or five shakes of Tabasco. Mix, cover, and turn heat off.

Turn fish over and continue to cook. Fish should be lightly browned.

Drain potatoes and return to pan. Pour melted mint butter over potatoes and mix to coat.

Drain liquid off spinach mixture.
Place halibut filets on warm plates, add mint potatoes and spinach mixture, and top spinach with grated Parmesan cheese.

Serve with wine.

Serves two.

To serve four, use four halibut filets, two bunches of spinach, four Roma tomatoes, and four potatoes. Follow the same directions.

#   Shrimp Newburg Flambéed in Brandy

*Shrimp sautéed in butter, then flambéed in brandy and blended with cream, egg yolks, and Dijon mustard. Served on rice cooked in chicken stock with garlic, clove, and onions, with a mushroom sauté. Recommended wine: Chardonnay.*

---

**Total time: 50 minutes**

### Ingredients

| | |
|---|---|
| 10 | to 12 mushrooms |
| 12 | large shrimp |
| 1 | Spanish onion |
| | Fresh parsley |
| 1 | small white onion |
| 4 | whole cloves |
| 1 | clove garlic |
| 1 | cup long-grain rice |
| | Butter |
| | Salt |
| 1¾ | cups chicken stock |
| ¼ | teaspoon curry |
| 1 | cup heavy cream |
| 2 | egg yolks |
| | Cayenne pepper |
| 3 | ounces brandy |
| 1 | teaspoon Dijon mustard |

### Utensils needed

Two skillets, pan.

---

Once started, follow recipe through to the end without stopping.

Place two wine glasses in freezer to chill.
Preheat oven to 200 degrees.

Wash mushrooms, cut off stems, and discard. Set caps aside.
Peel shrimp, cut each in half lengthwise, and set aside.
Peel and dice Spanish onion, then set aside.
Chop 1 teaspoon parsley, and set aside.
Skin white onion and cut in half. Pierce each half with two whole cloves, and set aside.
Peel 1 clove garlic.

Wash 1 cup rice in cold water several times. Cover with water and let sit.

In a pan, melt 3 tablespoons butter over medium heat.

Set the table.

Add both white onion halves and garlic clove to melted butter. Sauté 5 minutes.
Drain rice and add to onion butter. Cook 5 minutes, stirring occasionally.
Add a pinch of salt, 1¾ cups chicken stock, and ¼ teaspoon curry.
Cover and bring to a boil, then reduce heat to low.

In a bowl, blend together 1 cup cream, 2 egg yolks, chopped parsley, and a pinch of cayenne pepper.

In a skillet, melt 2 tablespoons butter over medium heat. Add Spanish onion, and sauté until onion is just wilted. Add shrimp, stir, and cook until shrimp is pink on both sides.

While shrimp cooks, in a second skillet melt 2 tablespoons butter over medium heat.
Add mushrooms and toss to coat mushrooms with butter.

To shrimp add 3 ounces brandy and carefully ignite at side of skillet with match. Shake skillet, stirring until all flame is gone. *(The alcohol from the brandy burns with a blue flame that is very hot and hard to see. Be careful not to reach across skillet.)*

Add cream-egg mixture and stir well. Add 1 teaspoon Dijon mustard and mix. Reduce heat to low.

Place two ovenproof plates in oven to warm.
Seat your guests.
Open wine and serve.

Remove plates from oven.
Place rice on plate, and top rice with shrimp mixture. Garnish with parsley.
Add mushrooms and serve.

Serves two.

To serve four, use 20 large shrimp and 18 mushrooms. For sauce, use 1½ cups cream, 3 eggs, and 2 teaspoons Dijon mustard. Follow the same directions.

# Sautéed Swordfish with Hot Cucumber Pepper Relish

*Swordfish steaks sautéed in butter, with a hot cucumber, onion, red pepper, and mint relish. Served with an escarole, Romaine, tomato salad with crumbled Roquefort cheese, and a baked asparagus and Swiss cheese casserole. Recommended wine: Gewurztraminer.*

| Total time: 60 minutes |
| --- |

## Ingredients

½ teaspoon Dijon mustard
  Salt and pepper
5 tablespoons vinegar
  Olive oil
1 bunch asparagus
1 cup Swiss cheese
1 cucumber
1 small onion
1 red pepper
2 cloves garlic
6 or 7 sprigs fresh mint
  Butter
2 eggs
1 tablespoon paprika
½ teaspoon cayenne
¼ teaspoon cinnamon
2 teaspoons sugar
2 swordfish steaks (about ¾ inch thick)
  Escarole
  Romaine lettuce
1 large tomato
  Roquefort cheese

## Utensils needed

Pot with lid, vegetable steamer, large skillet, small baking dish.

Once started, follow recipe through to the end without stopping.

Heat oven to 350 degrees.
Place two wine glasses in freezer to chill.

Prepare vegetable steamer with water and place over high heat.

In a bowl, mix ½ teaspoon Dijon mustard, ½ teaspoon salt, ¼ teaspoon pepper, and 2 tablespoons vinegar. Whisk in 5 tablespoons olive oil and set aside.

Cut asparagus tips 6 inches long and add to vegetable steamer. Cover and cook over high heat.

Grate 1 cup Swiss cheese, loosely packed, and set aside.
Peel cucumber, cut in half, and seed, then dice into ¼-inch cubes. (*Use spoon to scrape seeds out of center of cucumber.*) Toss cucumber with ½ teaspoon salt. Place in strainer and let drain.
Peel onion and dice into ¼-inch pieces. Set aside.
Cut red pepper in half, seed, and dice into ¼-inch pieces. Set aside. (*When seeding pepper, be sure to remove the white membrane because it tends to be bitter. See Tips and Techniques for easy dicing.*)

Remove asparagus tips from steamer, drain, and let cool.

Peel 2 cloves garlic and crush with side of knife. Set aside.

Strip mint leaves from six or seven sprigs of mint and chop leaves. (*To chiffonade and chop leaves, see Tips and Techniques.*)

In a skillet, heat 2 tablespoons olive oil over medium-high heat.

Butter small baking dish.
In a bowl, beat 2 eggs with 1 tablespoon paprika and 1 cup grated Swiss cheese.

Place asparagus tips in baking dish with all tips facing the same way. Pour egg and cheese mixture over top. Place in oven.

Add onions and red pepper to oil, and cook until onion just starts to brown.

While onions cook, set the table.

Add garlic to skillet with onions and peppers, and stir. Add cucumbers, ½ teaspoon cayenne, ¼ teaspoon cinnamon, 2 teaspoons sugar, and 3 tablespoons vinegar. Cook until liquid has evaporated. Add chopped mint leaves, remove from heat, and transfer to bowl.

In the same skillet, melt 2 tablespoons butter over medium-high heat. *(Do not allow butter to burn.)* Lightly salt both sides of swordfish steaks and sauté in butter until they just start to brown (about 5 minutes).

While fish cooks, chop enough escarole and Romaine lettuce to make salad for two. Place in bowl and toss.
Slice tomato and set aside.

Turn fish over and continue cooking.

Crumble Roquefort cheese into salad dressing to taste, and mix.
Place salad greens on salad plates. Top with tomato slices and spoon dressing over top.

Turn off oven and place two ovenproof plates in oven to warm.

Turn fish over.
Return cucumber mixture to skillet with swordfish, and mix.

Remove asparagus from oven and let stand.

When cucumber mixture is hot, remove plates from oven. Place swordfish steak on plate and top with cucumber relish. Garnish with a sprig of mint. Add asparagus to plate and serve with salad and wine.

Serves two.

To serve four, use four swordfish steaks, and follow the same directions.

# Beef and Pork Dinners

Filet Mignon Flambéed in Brandy with Mustard Cream Sauce

Individual Beef Wellingtons

Beef Stroganoff on a Bed of Egg Noodles

Beef Stew Bourguignonne on Sherry Rice

Broiled Beef Loin Steak with Horseradish Sauce

Baked Ham with Mushrooms and Onions in a
Honey Wine Sauce

Sautéed Pork Tenderloin with Cherry Sauce

Parmesan-Breaded Pork Chops in Mustard Cream Sauce

Sweet-and-Sour Pork with Sesame Fried Rice

Beef Fajitas with Cheddar Cheese Corn Polenta

# 🎗 Filet Mignon Flambéed in Brandy with Mustard Cream Sauce

Tender filet mignon sautéed in butter, then flambéed in brandy and topped with an onion, cream, Dijon mustard sauce. Served with boiled potato balls, and steamed, julienne zucchini and summer squash. Recommended wine: Cabernet Sauvignon.

---

| Total time: 50 minutes |
| --- |

## Ingredients

1 zucchini
1 yellow crookneck squash
4 large mushrooms
2 potatoes
1 small white onion
¼ cup brandy
1 cup heavy cream
⅛ cup Dijon mustard
   Butter
2 filet mignon

## Utensils needed

Vegetable steamer and pan, two skillets, pot, melon baller.

---

Once started, follow recipe through to the end without stopping.

Preheat oven to 300 degrees.

Cut zucchini in half lengthwise. Scrape out seeds with spoon. Cut into ⅛-inch-wide strips, 3 inches long. Repeat same process with yellow squash. (*All strips should be the same thickness. This will allow even cooking of all vegetables.*)

Prepare vegetable steamer, and place zucchini and squash in steamer. Do not turn on heat.

Wash mushrooms, cut off stems, and discard. Set mushroom caps aside.

Peel potatoes. With large end of melon baller, cut balls out of potatoes. (*Each potato should yield 6 to 7 potato balls. If you don't have a melon baller, dice potatoes into ½-inch squares. See Tips and Techniques.*)
Place 1 quart of water in pot, salt, and place potato balls in water. Do not turn on heat.

Finely dice 2 tablespoons onion, and set aside.
Measure ¼ cup brandy, and set aside.
Measure 1 cup heavy cream, and set aside.
Measure ⅛ cup Dijon mustard, and set aside.

In a skillet, melt 1 tablespoon butter over medium heat. Trim fat from filets, then salt and pepper both sides.
Sauté filets in butter for 15 minutes, turning frequently.

While filets sauté, set the table.

When filets are cooked, turn potatoes to high heat.
Pour brandy over filets and carefully ignite at side of skillet. Shake skillet until all flame dies. (*An alcohol flame is light blue and hard to see. To avoid burns, make sure you don't reach across skillet until all flame is gone. For a dramatic flare, you could turn out the lights when you flambé.*)

Turn zucchini to high heat.

Remove filets to platter and place in oven. Cook diced onion in brandy drippings about 3 minutes. Stir in 1 cup whipping cream and cook until slightly thickened.
Add Dijon mustard and stir. Reduce heat to medium low.

Add mushroom caps to zucchini, cover, and continue to cook.

Mix ½ tablespoon cornstarch with 1 tablespoon water. Add to cream sauce and stir until mixture thickens.
Reduce heat to low, stirring occasionally. *(If sauce is too thick, thin with water, adding 1 tablespoon at a time.)*

Open wine and allow to breathe. *(Breathing will allow the wine to open up and the flavors to enhance.)*

In a second skillet, melt 2 tablespoons butter over medium heat.
Drain potatoes and add to butter. Toss to coat potato balls on all sides.

Place two ovenproof plates in oven to warm.

Set background music, and seat your guest.

Turn off zucchini. *(Zucchini should be soft on the outside, with a slight crunch in the center.)*
Stir cream sauce.

Remove plates from oven. Place filet on each plate. Spoon cream sauce over filet, and top each with two mushroom caps.
Add zucchini, squash, add potato balls to plate, and serve.

Serves two.

To serve four, use two zucchini, two squash, eight mushrooms, four potatoes, and four filet mignon. Follow the same directions.

# ✿ Individual Beef Wellingtons

Seared filet mignon wrapped in puff pastry, egg-washed, and baked to a golden brown. Served with a creamed corn–sherry soup, and a spinach and vermicelli pasta sautéed with Parmesan cheese. Recommended wine: Merlot.

---

| **Total time: 60 minutes** |
| --- |

## Ingredients

- 2  filet mignon, approximately 3 inches in diameter
- 2  tablespoons olive oil
- 1  can cream-style corn
- ½  cup cream
- 1  teaspoon sherry
- 2  green onions
- 8  ounces liverwurst, at room temperature
- 1  cup broken vermicelli pasta
- ⅓  cup grated fresh Parmesan cheese
- 1  cup grated cheddar cheese
- 1  clove garlic
- 1  bunch spinach
- 1  puff pastry sheet (thawed)
- 1  egg
    Nutmeg
    Butter

## Utensils needed

Baking sheet, small pan, large pan, two skillets.

---

Once started, follow recipe through to the end without stopping.

Preheat oven to 400 degrees.

Trim filets and form into 3-inch-diameter shape. Lightly salt and pepper filets. Sear filets in 2 tablespoons hot oil over medium-high heat. Drain on paper towel. *(Searing quickly cooks the outside edges and holds the juices inside.)*

Fill large pan with water and place over high heat.
Place creamed corn in small pan over low heat. Add ½ cup cream and 1 tablespoon sherry. Mix well.

Chop two green onions.
In a bowl, mix green onions and liverwurst, then set aside.

Break 1 cup vermicelli into 2-inch pieces, and set aside.
Finely grate ⅓ cup Parmesan cheese, and set aside.
Coarsely grate 1 cup lightly packed cheddar cheese, and set aside.
Mince 1 clove garlic, and set aside. *(To mince garlic, peel and crush clove with side of knife blade. With pressure on knife blade, rub blade across garlic in a rocking motion. See Tips and Techniques.)*

Grab several sections of spinach leaves where stems meet the leaves and twist off the stems. Repeat with all spinach. Wash leaves thoroughly. Set aside. *(Spinach is grown in sandy soil, and if not rinsed thoroughly, you will get a gritty texture when you eat it.)*

Add vermicelli to boiling water.

Spread top of filets with liverwurst mixture, about ¼ inch thick.

Carefully open one pastry sheet. *(If pastry is well chilled, be careful not to let it break while unfolding.)*
Roll out one sheet to a 16-inch square.
Cut pastry in quarters to form four 8-inch squares.
Place filet on pastry, liverwurst side down.
Fold pastry around filet, seal center edge with a little water, and press to form seam. Fold ends up, seal seams with a little water, and press together. Place seam-side down on baking sheet.

With excess pastry, cut a leaf shape. With back of knife, make an indent down the center, then small angled indents from center to edge, forming leaf pattern.

Beat egg in bowl. Brush Wellingtons with beaten egg. Place leaf on top and brush leaf with egg. Place in oven.

Set the table.

Drain vermicelli, and set aside.

Add 1 cup grated cheddar cheese to corn soup and stir until cheese melts.
Serve soup, topped with a sprinkle of nutmeg.

When soup course is finished (approximately 10 minutes), melt 1½ tablespoons butter in skillet over medium-high heat. Add chopped garlic and sauté a few seconds.
Add spinach leaves and stir to coat spinach with butter.
Cook spinach until completely wilted, stirring occasionally. Add spaghetti and mix.

Place two ovenproof plates in oven to warm.

Add half the Parmesan cheese to spinach and mix. Remove from heat.

Open wine and allow wine to breathe. *(This allows red wines to open and the flavors to become more complex.)*

Place Wellington on plate, add Parmesan spinach, top with remaining Parmesan cheese, and serve.

Serves two.

To serve four, serve soup in smaller bowls. Use two cups broken vermicelli, two bunches spinach, ⅓ cup Parmesan cheese, four filet mignon, and two sheets puff pastry (one package). Follow the same directions.

# 🍲 Beef Stroganoff on a Bed of Egg Noodles

Steak strips sautéed in garlic butter and simmered with cream, cream cheese, sautéed onions, Madeira, mushrooms, and sour cream. Served on egg noodles and accompanied by a radish salad with a vinegar, mustard, and chive dressing and blanched cauliflower dredged in flour and pan fried. Recommended wine: Cabernet Sauvignon.

| Total time: 60 minutes |
| --- |

## Ingredients

 2  eggs
 1  bunch radishes
 1  green pepper
 1  small can sliced black olives (2¼ ounces)
 1  bunch fresh chives
    Olive oil
 ¼  cup vinegar
 1  teaspoon sugar
 1  teaspoon dry mustard
    Salt and pepper
 1  cauliflower
 1  onion
 8  mushrooms
 ¾  pound flank steak
 2  cloves garlic
 ¼  cup Madeira or dry sherry
 3  ounces cream cheese
 6  ounces egg noodles
 1  head bib or butter lettuce
    Butter
 ½  cup flour
 1½ cups sour cream

## Utensils needed

Two skillets, pot, small pan.

Once started, follow recipe through to the end without stopping.

Fill small pan with hot water and place over high heat. Place eggs in water to hard boil.

Preheat oven to 250 degrees.

Cut ends from radishes and discard.
Wash radishes and slice thin. Place in large bowl and set aside.
Core and seed green pepper. Dice ¼ pepper and add to radishes. (*See Tips and Techniques section for way to easily seed and dice pepper.*)
Drain olives and add to radishes. Refrigerate.

Chop 3 tablespoons chives. In a bowl, whisk together ⅓ cup olive oil, ¼ cup vinegar, chives, 1 teaspoon sugar, 1 teaspoon dry mustard, ½ teaspoon salt, and ⅛ teaspoon pepper. Refrigerate.

Fill pot with hot water for cauliflower and place over high heat.
Cut flowerets from three-quarters of the cauliflower and cut into bite-size pieces. Set aside.

Skin and slice half the onion, and set aside.
Remove eggs from heat and let stand.
Wash mushrooms, slice caps, and set aside.
Slice flank steak across the grain into ¼-inch-thick slices. Set aside.

In one large skillet, over medium-high heat, add 1 tablespoon oil and 2 cloves crushed garlic. (*To crush garlic, see Tips and Techniques.*)

Set the table.

When water in pot boils, add cauliflower.

When garlic starts to sizzle, add flank steak strips, salt and pepper to taste, and sauté until meat is opaque on all sides, about 4 minutes, turning frequently. Remove steak to plate and place in oven to keep warm.

Drain almost all liquid from the same skillet meat was sautéed in, break onion slices apart, and sauté over medium heat until onions are soft.

Drain cauliflower and set aside. Refill pot with hot water for egg noodles. Add 1 tablespoon oil, salt, and return to high heat. Do not add noodles.

In a second skillet, melt 2 tablespoons butter over medium-high heat.

Drain hard-boiled eggs and run under cold water. Peel hard-boiled eggs. Chop eggs and set aside.

Stir onions.

Place ½ cup flour in zip-lock bag. Add cauliflower in small batches, and shake bag to dust cauliflower with flour. Shake off excess flour. Add cauliflower to melted butter, and shake skillet to coat on all sides. Sauté until lightly browned.

Open wine and allow to breathe.

Place one lettuce leaf on each salad plate. Slice remaining lettuce and mix with radishes. Place salad in lettuce leaf. Whisk chive dressing and spoon dressing over salad. Top with chopped egg and refrigerate.

When water boils, add 8 ounces noodles.

Toss cauliflower, browning on all sides.

Add mushrooms to sautéed onions and mix.
Add ¼ cup Madeira and 3 ounces cream cheese, cut into chunks. Mix until cheese is melted and blended and mixture is hot.

Place two ovenproof plates in oven to warm. *(Warmed plates will keep food warm for a longer time, giving you more time to serve.)*

Add meat to onion-mushroom mixture. Let heat a few minutes.
Add 1½ cups sour cream, blend, and heat.

Drain noodles when done. *(To test, noodles should have a slight resistance when bitten. This is* al dente.*)* Rinse under hot water, and let drain again. Place noodles on warm plate and top with stroganoff mixture. Add sautéed cauliflower. Serve with radish salad.

Serves two.

To serve four, use 3 eggs, 2 bunches radishes, ½ green pepper, diced, all the cauliflower, 1½ pounds flank steak, 3 cloves garlic, ½ cup Madeira, 8 ounces cream cheese, 12 ounces egg noodles, and 2 cups sour cream. Follow the same directions.

# ❧ Beef Stew Bourguignonne on Sherry Rice

Cubed London broil marinated in red wine and garlic, simmered with bacon, beef broth, red wine, carrots, mushrooms, onion, leeks, and potatoes. Served over sherry-flavored rice with fresh French bread. Recommended wine: Zinfandel.

---

Total time: 60 minutes

---

### Ingredients

1   small London broil, approximately ½ pound
½   cup soy sauce
    Red cooking wine (Burgundy)
3   cloves garlic
1   teaspoon thyme
6   mushrooms
2   to 3 carrots
6   white boiling (pearl) onions
2   potatoes
1   leek
1   piece suet (optional and available from your butcher)
3   strips bacon
    Olive oil
1   cup flour
2   tablespoons sugar
1   14-ounce can beef broth
1   tablespoon sage
½   cup sherry
1   cup white rice
    Salt and pepper
    French bread

### Utensils needed

Skillet, pan with cover, pot with cover.

---

Once started, follow recipe through to the end without stopping.

Preheat oven to 250 degrees.

Cut meat into ½-inch cubes, place in bowl, and add ½ cup soy sauce, ½ cup red wine, 1 clove crushed garlic, and 1 teaspoon thyme. *(See Tips and Techniques for easy ways to peel and crush garlic.)* Mix and set aside.

In a skillet, over medium-high heat, add suet and bacon. Cook until rendered and lightly browned.

In a pot, over medium heat, place 1 cup beef broth, 1 cup red wine, and 1 tablespoon sage.

Wash mushrooms and slice caps ¼ inch thick. Set aside. *(Make sure all slices are the same thickness to ensure even cooking of all vegetables.)*
Peel carrots and slice ⅛ inch thick, then set aside.
Skin onions, and set aside.
Trim root and green end from leek, slice down the center, and rinse under cold water, removing any sand or grit. Slice ¼ inch thick and set aside.
Peel potatoes and cut into ½ inch chunks, then set aside.

Place 1 cup flour and 2 tablespoons sugar in large zip-lock bag.

Add carrots, onions, leeks, and potatoes to wine-broth mixture. Do not add mushrooms.

Remove bacon and suet and discard. Add a thin layer of olive oil to skillet and let heat.
Peel 2 cloves garlic and slice thin. Set aside.

While oil heats, remove meat from marinade with slotted spoon, saving marinade. Shake meat in flour to coat. Let meat sit in flour bag.

Add garlic to oil. Cook until garlic just starts to brown.
While garlic browns, place 1 cup water and 1 cup sherry in pan, cover, and place over high heat.

Place meat in oil and cook until browned, turning frequently.

Place meat in pot with vegetables. Deglaze skillet by pouring remaining meat marinade into skillet and mixing to loosen brown bits on bottom. Add this to the pot, and add ½ teaspoon pepper and ¼ teaspoon salt. Cover and let cook.

Add 1 cup white rice to boiling water and reduce heat to simmer. Stir and cover.

Add mushrooms to bourguignonne stew mixture, stir, cover, and reduce heat to medium-low.

Set the table. Open wine and allow it to breathe.
Take a 5-minute break with your guest.

Place two ovenproof plates in oven to warm.

Remove rice from heat. Add 2 tablespoons sherry and stir to mix. Cover and let sit off heat.

Cut four slices of French bread, and set aside.

Mix 2 tablespoons flour with 3 tablespoons red wine to form a runny paste. Add this to stew a little at a time, stirring constantly until desired thickness is reached. (*If mixture does not thicken quickly, increase heat to medium and continue cooking until mixture thickens.*)

Remove plates from oven. Place rice on one side of plate. Spoon bourguignonne stew partially over rice and onto plate, making sure all ingredients are presented. Add French bread on the side and serve with wine.

Serves two.

To serve four, use ¾ pound London broil, 8 mushrooms, 8 onions, and 2 leeks. Add 1 additional cup of wine to vegetables. Follow the same directions.

## 🦐 Broiled Beef Loin Steak with Horseradish Sauce

Broiled beef loin steaks with a sour cream–horseradish sauce. Served with angel hair pasta in a Swiss cheese white sauce and with corn flavored with oregano. The appetizer is escargot in pesto butter with French bread. Recommended wine: Cabernet Sauvignon.

---

**Total time: 55 minutes**

---

### Ingredients

1   can escargot
3   cloves garlic
    Fresh parsley
1   French roll
¾   cup grated Swiss cheese
1   stick butter
1   package dry pesto mix (½ ounce)
    Olive oil
2   beef loin steaks, 1½ inches thick
¾   cup sour cream
3   tablespoons prepared horseradish
2   tablespoons butter
1   tablespoon flour
1   cup milk
1   can whole-kernel corn
1   teaspoon oregano
4   ounces angel hair pasta

---

### Utensils needed

Broiler pan, three sauce pans, pot.

---

Once started, follow recipe through to the end without stopping.

Drain and wash escargot, then set aside.
Peel and crush 3 cloves garlic, and set aside. (*Crush garlic clove with side of heavy knife, applying pressure with heel of hand. See Tips and Techniques for easy ways to peel and crush garlic.*)
Finely dice 1 tablespoon parsley, and set aside.
Slice French roll into ¼-inch-thick slices.
Grate ¾ cup Swiss cheese, and set aside.

Melt one stick butter in sauce pan over medium heat.
While butter melts, set the table.

Add 1 package pesto mix to butter and blend well. Remove from heat and blend in 1 tablespoon olive oil. Add crushed garlic and escargot and let stand.

Rub steaks with olive oil on both sides, salt and pepper, place on broiler pan, and set aside.

In a bowl, combine ¾ cup sour cream and 3 tablespoons horseradish. Blend well and transfer to a serving dish. Refrigerate.

In a second sauce pan, melt 2 tablespoons butter over medium heat.

In a pot, place 2 quarts water over high heat for pasta. Salt the water and add 1 tablespoon olive oil. (*Oil prevents pasta from sticking together.*)

Return escargot to medium heat and stir.
To melted butter add 1 tablespoon flour and blend with whisk. (*This makes a roux, which is the thickening agent in many sauces.*) Add ½ cup milk and whisk until mixture is smooth. Remove from heat.

Turn oven to broil and place steaks in broiler approximately 4 inches from heat source.

Drain corn and place in pan. Add 1 teaspoon oregano and mix. Place over medium-low heat.

Place several French bread slices on small plate, spoon escargot in center, top with sauce, and serve.

After escargot course (approximately 10 minutes), turn steaks and return to broiler.
Stir corn.

Add 4 ounces angel hair pasta to boiling water.
Return white sauce to medium-low heat, add grated Swiss cheese, and blend. Add ½ cup milk and blend.

Take a short break with your guest while pasta cooks, about 4 to 5 minutes.

Turn broiler off.
Place two ovenproof plates in oven to warm.
Stir white sauce.
Drain pasta. Add pasta to cheese mixture and stir to coat well.
Place steak on warm plate, add pasta, and garnish with minced parsley. Add corn, then serve with horseradish sauce.

Serves two.

To serve four, use two cans escargot (24) and four steaks. For Swiss cheese sauce, use 3 tablespoons butter with 2 tablespoons flour. Blend in 1 cup milk and add 1½ cups grated Swiss cheese. Follow the same directions.

# ❦ Baked Ham with Mushrooms and Onions in a Honey Wine Sauce

*A small ham coated with brown sugar, honey, and cinnamon, surrounded with diced onions and mushrooms, then baked in white wine. Served with buttered yams and green peas. Recommended wine: Pinot Noir Blanc.*

| |
|---|
| **Total time: 40 minutes** |

## Ingredients

1   onion
4   large mushrooms
1   1½-pound canned ham
    (Armor Star™)
    Cinnamon
    Butter
    Honey
    Brown sugar
    White cooking wine
1   package frozen peas
    (10 ounces)
1   can yams
    Parsley

## Utensils needed

Small baking dish for ham, two sauce pans.

Once started, follow recipe through to the end without stopping.

Place two wine glasses in freezer to chill.

Turn oven to 350 degrees.

Dice half the onion, and set aside. *(To dice an onion easily, cut onion in half. Lay flat side on counter and make horizontal slices ¼ inch apart almost all the way through. Now make vertical slices ¼ inch apart. Slice across cuts ¼ inch apart and the onion is diced. See Tips and Techniques.)*

Clean mushrooms, remove the stems, and discard. Slice caps, and set aside.

Remove ham from container. Wash excess gelatin from ham and pat dry with paper towels. Sprinkle all sides of ham with cinnamon. Butter the baking dish. *(Baking dish should be just large enough to hold ham.)* Place ham in baking dish and coat sides and top with honey. Sprinkle generously with brown sugar, coating top and sides of ham. Pour 1 cup white cooking wine around, not over, ham. *(If baking dish is a larger size, you may need to add more wine.)* Add mushrooms and onion around ham and place in oven.

Fill pan with water for peas and place over medium-high heat.

Set the table, and set background music.
Take a 10-minute break with your guest.

Place peas in boiling water.
Place yams in sauce pan and add 2 tablespoons butter. Place over medium heat.
Take a 5-minute break with your guest.

Place two ovenproof plates in oven to warm.

Seat your guest and serve the wine. *(Don't forget the chilled glasses.)*

Remove ham from baking dish. Slice ham and place two slices on each plate. Spoon sauce with mushrooms and onion over ham. Place yams on plate and sprinkle with cinnamon. Add peas to plate, garnish with parsley, and serve.

Serves two.

To serve four, add one can of yams, and follow the same directions. You will have enough ham and sauce for four.

# Sautéed Pork Tenderloins with Cherry Sauce

Medallions of pork tenderloin dredged in flour and sautéed, topped with a thick cherry sauce. Served with rice cooked in chicken stock and simmered carrots, celery, onion, and apples, with a salad of Romaine, Swiss cheese, and garlic in a lemon-oil dressing. Recommended wine: Gamay Beaujolais.

---

**Total time: 55 minutes**

## Ingredients

1 head Romaine lettuce
1 bunch radishes
3 cloves garlic
1 small can chopped olives
1 large tomato
   Olive oil
1 tablespoon lemon juice
½ teaspoon dry mustard
   Salt and pepper
6 pork tenderloin slices (¾-inch-thick, 1½- to 2-inch rounds)
2 cups chicken stock
1 package Uncle Ben's™ long-grain and wild rice (or any rice that cooks in 25 minutes)
2 carrots
1 stalk celery
1 red apple
1 white onion
2 tablespoon butter
1 can cherry pie filling
⅓ cup flour
   Swiss cheese
¼ teaspoon nutmeg

## Utensils needed

Small pan, two medium pans, skillet.

Once started, follow recipe through to the end without stopping.

Preheat oven to 250 degrees.

Wash Romaine and slice enough for two salads. Place in bowl. Wash and thin slice four radishes. Add to lettuce.

Mince 1 clove garlic and add to lettuce. (*To mince garlic, crush with side of knife and, putting pressure on blade, rub blade back and forth over garlic in a rocking motion. See Tips and Techniques.*)

Drain olives and add to lettuce.
Dice tomato and add to lettuce. Toss to mix well, then refrigerate.

For salad dressing, in a small bowl, combine 3 tablespoons olive oil, 1 tablespoon lemon juice, ½ teaspoon dry mustard, ¼ teaspoon salt, and ¼ teaspoon pepper. Mix well and refrigerate.

Mince 2 cloves garlic and rub both sides of pork tenderloins with garlic. Lightly salt and pepper tenderloins and set aside.

Place 2 cups chicken stock in medium sauce pan. Add 1 cup of rice. Cover, and place over medium-high heat.

Peel carrots, slice them ⅛ inch thick and place in medium pan. (*Slice carrots on the diagonal for larger slices and better plate coverage. See Tips and Techniques.*)

Slice celery ⅛ inch thick and add to carrots. (*Slice celery on a diagonal also.*)

Core the apple, cut it into eight sections, and add to carrots. Set aside.
Peel and slice half the onion, and add to carrots. Add enough hot water to just cover vegetables. Add 1 tablespoon butter, cover, and place over medium heat.

Set the table.

Turn rice to low heat.

Place 1 tablespoon olive oil in skillet and place over medium-high heat.

Place cherry pie filling in small pan and place over medium-low heat.

Add apple sections to carrots.
Take a 5-minute break with your guest.

Place flour in a zip-lock baggie, add tenderloins, and shake to coat with flour. Shake off excess flour.

Reduce heat under oil to medium, add pork tenderloins to hot oil, and sear on both sides. Continue to cook, turning frequently, for 8 minutes.

While pork cooks, open the red wine and allow it to breathe.

Place two ovenproof plates in oven to warm. *(Serving on warm plates keeps the food hot 30 percent longer than on cold china.)*

Grate ½ cup Swiss cheese.
Place salad on plates, stir dressing, and spoon over salad. Sprinkle with grated Swiss cheese and refrigerate.
Seat your guest.

Drain vegetables. Remove apple sections and return vegetables to pan. Add 1 tablespoon butter and ¼ teaspoon nutmeg, and stir to melt butter.

Remove plates from oven, spoon some cherry sauce on plate, top with three tenderloins and spoon desired amount of cherry sauce over top. Add vegetables to plate. Place two to three apple sections on plate, skin-side down, and add rice. Serve with salad.

Serves two.

To serve four, make four salads and double the ingredients in salad dressing. Use twelve pork tenderloin slices, two carrots, two celery stalks, and two apples. Grate one cup Swiss cheese. Follow the same directions.

# Parmesan-Breaded Pork Chops in Mustard Cream Sauce

*Thick pork chops breaded with Parmesan cheese and seasoned bread crumbs, then oven baked. Served with a creamy Dijon mustard sauce and rice pilaf with apple sauce flavored with rum. Recommended wine: Merlot.*

| Total time: 40 minutes |
| --- |

### Ingredients

2 cups chicken stock
2½ tablespoons butter
1 can apple sauce
3 tablespoons rum
1 cup rice pilaf, or any rice that cooks in 25 minutes
½ cup seasoned bread crumbs
1½ tablespoons Parmesan cheese
½ teaspoon basil
Olive oil
2 to 4 pork loin center cuts, depending on size, 1 inch thick
1½ tablespoons flour
1 cup cream
1 teaspoon dry mustard
2 tablespoons Dijon mustard
Cinnamon

### Utensils needed

Small pan, medium pan with cover, skillet.

Once started, follow recipe through to the end without stopping.

Preheat oven to 250 degrees.

Place 2 cups chicken stock in medium pan with 1 tablespoon butter. Cover and place over high heat.
Place apple sauce in bowl and add 3 tablespoons rum. Mix well, and refrigerate.

Set the table.

Add 1 cup rice pilaf to boiling chicken stock and stir. Cover pilaf and reduce heat to low.

In a bowl, combine ½ cup seasoned bread crumbs, 1½ tablespoons Parmesan cheese, and ½ teaspoon basil. Mix well and set aside.

Place 2 tablespoons olive oil in skillet over medium heat.

Take a 10-minute break with your guest.

In a small pan, melt 1½ tablespoons butter over medium heat.

Brush both sides of pork chops with olive oil, drop in breading, and coat well on all sides. Add breaded chops to hot oil.

To melted butter, whisk in 1½ tablespoons flour, and cook a few seconds. Whisk in ½ cup cream and blend until smooth. Add remaining cream and whisk.

Turn pork over and continue to cook.

Place two ovenproof plates in oven to warm.

Whisk sauce and cook until thickened and smooth. Reduce heat to low. Add 1 teaspoon dry mustard, 2 tablespoons Dijon mustard, and ⅓ cup hot water. Mix well.

Open the wine and allow it to breathe.

Turn pork skillet off and remove from heat.
Remove plates from oven. Spoon desired amount of sauce on plate and place pork chop in sauce. Add rice to plate. Place apple sauce in two small bowls, and sprinkle top with cinnamon. Serve.

Serves two.

To serve four, use 8 to 12 pork loin cuts. For breading, use 1 cup seasoned bread crumbs, 3 tablespoons Parmesan cheese, and 1 teaspoon basil. Follow the same directions.

# ❀ Sweet-and-Sour Pork with Sesame Fried Rice

*Egg-dipped, battered pork loin strips sautéed in oil and blended with a sweet-and-sour sauce of ginger, garlic, brown sugar, vinegar, soy sauce, and pineapple chunks. Served with simmered celery root and tomatoes and with white rice fried in dark sesame oil. Recommended wine: Pinot Noir.*

---

**Total time: 55 minutes**

## Ingredients

1   onion
1   celery root
1   clove garlic
1   bell pepper
2   tomatoes
    Butter
1   pork loin
2   tablespoons sherry
¼   cup flour
¼   cup cornstarch
2   tablespoons olive oil
1   teaspoon ginger
¼   cup vinegar
¼   cup chicken stock
3   tablespoons ketchup
¼   cup brown sugar
2   teaspoons soy sauce
1   cup pineapple
    chunks
1   cup white rice
    (that cooks in 25
    minutes)
1   egg
    Dark sesame oil

## Utensils needed

Two skillets, two medium pans with covers, small pan.

Once started, follow recipe through to the end without stopping.

Preheat oven to 350 degrees.

Place 2 cups water in medium pan, and place over high heat.

Dice ½ onion, and set aside. *(See Tips and Techniques for dicing.)*

Peel celery root, and slice into ⅛-inch-thick slices. Cut slices in half, and set aside. *(Be sure all slices are the same thickness.)*

Mince 1 clove garlic, and set aside.

Medium dice half the bell pepper, and set aside. *(Medium dice is ¼-inch cubes. To seed and dice a pepper easily, see Tips and Techniques.)*

Cut an X in the bottom of tomatoes and drop in boiling water for 35 seconds. Immediately drain. Peel tomatoes by pulling skin at points of X cuts.

Place 2 cups water in a pan and add 1 tablespoon butter. Place over high heat.

Cut pork loin into ½-inch-square strips about 4 inches long. Cut 8 to 10 strips. Place pork strips in bowl, and add 2 tablespoons sherry. Mix to coat and set aside.

Mix ¼ cup flour with ¼ cup cornstarch in bowl, and set aside.

In a second medium pan, add 1½ cups water, 1 tablespoon butter, sliced celery root, ¼ teaspoon salt, and ¼ teaspoon pepper. Cover and place over medium-low heat.

In a small pan, add 1 tablespoon olive oil, place over medium-high heat and add minced garlic, diced onion, and 1 teaspoon ginger. Sauté until onion starts to brown. Add ¼ cup vinegar, ¼ cup chicken stock, 3 tablespoons ketchup, ¼ cup brown sugar, 2 teaspoons soy sauce, 1 cup pineapple chunks, and diced pepper. Stir to mix, and reduce heat to medium.

Add 1 cup rice to boiling water, stir, cover, and turn heat to low.

Set the table.
Take a 15-minute break with your guest.

Add sliced tomatoes to celery root. Cover and continue to cook.

Place 2 tablespoons oil in skillet over medium heat.
Beat egg in small bowl and add to pork strips. Mix to coat all pork. Dredge pork in flour mixture, coating all sides well. Place pork on plate and let stand.

In a second skillet, melt 2 tablespoons butter over medium-high heat. Remove rice from heat. When butter is foaming, add rice to skillet and stir. Add 2 tablespoons sesame oil, stir, and let cook.

Place pork strips in hot oil.

Mix 2½ teaspoons cornstarch with 1½ teaspoons water. Add to sweet-and-sour sauce and stir to thicken.
Place two ovenproof plates in oven to warm.
Stir rice and continue to cook.

When pork is lightly browned on one side, turn over.

Open the wine and allow it to breathe.

Drain celery root and tomatoes.
Remove plates from oven. Place small amount of sweet-and-sour sauce on plate, place four pork strips on sauce, and spoon additional sauce over top. Add rice to plate. Add celery root and tomatoes, and serve.

Serves two.

To serve four, cut 16 to 20 pork loin strips, and dice whole onion. For sweet-and-sour sauce, use 2 teaspoons ginger, ½ cup vinegar, ½ cup chicken stock, 6 tablespoons ketchup, ½ cup brown sugar, 1 tablespoon soy sauce, and 2 cups pineapple chunks. Follow the same directions.

# ❧ Beef Fajitas with Cheddar Cheese Corn Polenta

Strips of beef marinated in lime juice and garlic, then sautéed in butter and served over sautéed onions, green peppers, and tomatoes, seasoned with oregano, rosemary, and basil. Served with mashed bean patties with red pepper flakes, and cheddar cheese corn polenta. Recommended wine: Zinfandel.

---

**Total time: 60 minutes**

### Ingredients

- 2 limes
- Olive oil
- 6 cloves garlic
- 2 skirt steaks (¾ pound total)
- 1 large white onion
- 1 green pepper
- 1 red pepper
- 1 14.5-ounce can chopped tomatoes
- 1 teaspoon oregano
- 1 teaspoon rosemary
- 1 teaspoon basil
- Salt and pepper
- 2½ cups chicken stock
- 1 can kidney beans
- Tabasco
- Nutmeg
- 2 eggs
- 1 tablespoon cream
- ½ teaspoon red pepper flakes
- Butter
- ¾ pound sharp cheddar cheese
- ¾ cup corn meal

### Utensils needed

Two skillets, pan, small baking dish.

Once started, follow recipe through to the end without stopping.

Preheat oven to 325 degrees.

Juice limes and place juice in bowl. (*Rolling limes on a counter while applying pressure with heel of hand will loosen the juice before cutting and squeezing out the juice.*) Add 1½ tablespoons olive oil to juice.
Crush 2 cloves garlic and add to lime juice. (*Crush peeled cloves with side of knife blade. See Tips and Techniques.*)
Cut skirt steaks into ¼-inch-thick slices. Sprinkle with pepper on both sides. Place in lime juice and mix to coat all meat well. Set aside.

Medium dice onion, and set aside. (*Medium dice is ¼-inch cubes. See Tips and Techniques for onion-dicing tips.*)

Place ¼ cup olive oil in skillet over medium-high heat.

Remove seeds from peppers, and medium dice them. Set aside. (*See Tips and Techniques for instruction to seed and dice peppers easily.*)

Puree four cloves garlic with side of knife. (*Adding salt to cutting board before crushing clove will act as an abrasive. Then run side of knife blade across garlic in a rocking motion while applying pressure with heel of hand. This will puree garlic. See Tips and Techniques.*)

Add garlic and onion to hot oil, and sauté until onion is transparent.

While onion cooks, set the table.
Stir onions and add peppers, tomatoes, and juice. Add 1 teaspoon oregano, 1 teaspoon rosemary, and 1 teaspoon basil. Salt and pepper to taste and mix well. Reduce heat to low.

In a pan, bring 2 ½ cups chicken stock to boil over high heat.

Drain kidney beans. Mash beans in bowl with potato masher or fork. Add 3 shakes Tabasco and ¼ teaspoon nutmeg, and mix well. Separate two egg yolks, add to mashed beans, and mix. Add

2 tablespoons cream and ½ teaspoon red pepper flakes, and mix well. Butter small baking dish. With spoon, drop equal amounts of bean mixture into baking dish, making four patties. Place in oven.

Stir pepper mixture.
Grate 1½ cups cheddar cheese, and set aside.

Take a 5-minute break with your guest.

In a second skillet, melt 2 tablespoons butter over medium heat.

When chicken stock is boiling, remove from heat and gradually stir in 1 cup corn meal, whisking to avoid lumps. Add grated cheese and mix to melt cheese. Place over medium-low heat and continue cooking.

Place two ovenproof plates in oven to warm.

When butter is hot, sauté beef strips on one side for 2 minutes.

Stir pepper mixture.
Stir polenta.

Turn beef strips and sauté other side for 2 minutes. Remove from heat.
Remove polenta from heat and let stand.

Remove plates from oven.
Spoon pepper mixture on plates, and top with beef strips.
Add cheese polenta and bean patties to plates and serve with wine.

Serves two.

To serve four, use four skirt steaks. You should have enough pepper mixture, polenta, and bean patties. Follow the same directions.

Mixed Lamb English Grill, Carrot Fritters, and Mashed Potatoes with Brown Gravy  (page 108).

Individual Beef Wellingtons with Spinach and Vermicelli Pasta Sauté and Creamed Corn–Sherry Soup (page 68).

Apricot Honey Chicken with Mandarin Oranges, Brown Rice with Peas and Mushrooms (page 30).

Almond-Battered Fried Halibut, Mint-Buttered Potatoes, and Spinach, Corn, and Tomato Sauté (page 58).

# Veal Dinners

Veal Chops Cordon Bleu

Veal Chops Baked in Sour Cream and Mushrooms

Stuffed Veal Rolls with Vegetable Sauce

Veal Bourguignonne on a Bed of Pasta

Veal Scaloppine in Mushroom Gravy on Rice

Veal Parmigiana on a Bed of Pasta

Breaded Veal Scaloppine with Olive Tomato Sauce

Veal Marsala with Fettuccine Alfredo

# 🌀 Veal Chops Cordon Bleu

Veal chops stuffed with cheese and ham, egg-dipped and breaded in seasoned bread crumbs, then oven baked. Served with sweet-and-sour red cabbage with apples and buttered spaetzel (small Swiss-style dumplings). Recommended wine: Gamay Beaujolais.

---

**Total time: 55 minutes**

### Ingredients

2 large, thick veal chops (4 if chops are small)
2 thin slices Swiss cheese
2 thin slices ham
2 eggs
  Flour
1 cup fine seasoned bread crumbs
  Olive oil
1 small red cabbage
1 apple
  Butter
  Salt and pepper
½ teaspoon nutmeg
2 tablespoons white vinegar
2 tablespoons brown sugar
1 lemon
1 package spaetzel
  Fresh parsley

### Utensils needed

Two sauce pans, baking dish.

---

Once started, follow recipe through to the end without stopping.

Preheat oven to 350 degrees.

Cut a pocket in the side of each chop. Sprinkle salt in pocket, and tuck 1 slice Swiss cheese and 1 slice ham into each pocket.
Beat two eggs in a bowl with fork.
Dust chops with flour, dip in egg, and coat all sides with bread crumbs.
Place 2 tablespoons olive oil in baking dish, add chops, and place in oven.

Shred ½ cabbage about ¼ inch thick, and set aside.
Core and dice apple into ¼-inch squares, and set aside.
In a sauce pan, melt half a cube butter over medium heat. Add cabbage, salt, and pepper to taste.
Add ½ teaspoon nutmeg, 2 tablespoons vinegar, 2 tablespoons brown sugar, and apple. Mix well, cover pan, and reduce heat to medium-low.

Place 1 quart water in pan for spaetzel, and salt the water. Do not turn on heat.

Set the table.
Take a 10-minute break with your guest.

Turn spaetzel water to high heat.
Turn veal chops over and return to oven.
Stir cabbage, cover, and continue to cook.
Cut four thin slices from center of lemon, and set aside.

Set background music, and open the wine to breathe.

When spaetzel water boils, add ½ box of spaetzel, and stir.
Take a 5-minute break with your guest.

Place two ovenproof plates in oven to warm. *(Warm plates keep the food hot longer, giving you more time to serve dinner.)*
Seat your guest.

When spaetzel is tender, drain it.
Return spaetzel to pan and add 2 tablespoons butter. Stir to melt butter and coat spaetzel.

Remove plates from oven. Place veal chop on each plate, garnish with lemon slices and parsley. Add cabbage and spaetzel to plate and serve.

Serves two.

To serve four, use four veal chops, three-quarters of the cabbage, two apples, and a full box of spaetzel. Follow the same directions.

# 🦋 Veal Chops Baked in Sour Cream and Mushrooms

Boned veal chops, sautéed and blended with onions, mushrooms, Madeira, and sour cream, then baked, and garnished with chopped pimientos. Served with pasta twists sautéed with caraway seeds and cabbage, and flavored with white wine vinegar. Recommended wine: Merlot.

---

| | |
|---|---|
| **Total time: 50 minutes** | Once started, follow recipe through to the end without stopping. |

Heat oven to 350 degrees.

Bone the veal chops, and save the bones and trimmings.
Medium dice the onion, and set aside. (*Medium dice is ¼-inch cubes. See Tips and Techniques for dicing tips.*)
Cut stems from the mushrooms and discard. Slice mushroom caps, and set aside.
Dice 1 tablespoon pimientos, and set aside.
Core the cabbage and quarter it. Chop one quarter, and set aside.
Place 1 chicken bouillon cube in ⅓ cup hot water.
Place 1 quart water in pot for pasta, salt the water, and add 1 tablespoon oil. Do not turn on heat.

Melt 1 tablespoon butter in skillet over medium-high heat.
Add veal chops, bones, and trimmings. Sauté on both sides until brown. Remove veal steaks to baking dish, and discard bones and trimmings.

In the same skillet, reduce heat to medium and melt 1 tablespoon butter. Add 1 tablespoon diced onion and sauté 1 minute. Add sliced mushrooms and sauté 2 minutes longer.
Reduce heat to low and stir in 1 tablespoon flour.

Turn pasta water to high.

Add bouillon to mushroom mixture. (*Mixture will thicken as bouillon is stirred in.*) Add 2 tablespoons Madeira, ¾ cup sour cream, ½ teaspoon salt, and ½ teaspoon pepper, and mix well. Pour mixture over veal, cover with foil, and place in oven.

Melt 2 tablespoons butter in second skillet over medium heat.

Add 1½ cups pasta twists to boiling water.

Set the table.

## Ingredients

- 2 veal chops
- 1 onion
- ¼ pound mushrooms
- 1 small jar of pimientos
- 1 small cabbage
- 1 chicken bouillon cube
- 1 tablespoon cooking oil
- Salt and pepper
- Butter
- 1 tablespoon flour
- 2 tablespoons Madeira
- ¾ cup sour cream
- 1 package pasta twists
- 1 tablespoon caraway seeds
- 2 tablespoons white wine vinegar
- Fresh parsley

## Utensils needed

Two skillets, baking dish, pot.

Sauté ½ cup diced onion in butter until tender. Add chopped cabbage, and stir well.
Take a 5-minute break with your guest.

Stir cabbage.
Open the wine and allow it to breathe. *(The breathing allows the wine's flavors to intensify and meld together.)*

Check pasta.
Remove cabbage from heat and set aside.
Place two ovenproof plates in oven to warm.

When pasta is tender, remove from heat and drain. Return to pot and add cabbage mixture, 1 tablespoon caraway seeds, 1 tablespoon butter, and 2 tablespoons white wine vinegar. Mix well to melt butter.

Remove plates from oven. Place veal on each plate and spoon sauce over top. Sprinkle pimientos over sauce. Add pasta-cabbage mixture to plate, garnish with fresh parsley, and serve.

Serves two.

To serve four, double all ingredients and follow the same directions.

# 🕸 Stuffed Veal Rolls with Vegetable Sauce

Thin veal cutlets layered with ham slices and stuffed with sautéed onions, bread crumbs, and parsley, then rolled and poached in chicken stock and topped with a carrot-and-onion vegetable sauce. Served with steamed broccoli in lemon-garlic oil, and a spinach–red onion salad with bacon bits and fresh-grated Parmesan cheese. Recommended wine: Gamay Beaujolais.

---

| Total time: 60 minutes |
| --- |

## Ingredients

2  small white onions
   Fresh parsley
2  carrots
   Butter
4  medium veal cutlets
   Wax paper
1  can chicken stock
   (2½ cups)
¼  cup seasoned bread
   crumbs
   Salt and pepper
⅛  cup heavy cream
4  thin slices ham
   String
1  bunch broccoli
1  bunch spinach
1  small red onion
3  tablespoons olive oil
1  tablespoon bacon bits
2  tablespoons
   Parmesan cheese
2  cloves garlic
1  lemon
1  cup white rice
1  tablespoon cornstarch

## Utensils needed

Two skillets, small baking dish, two pans, vegetable steamer.

---

Once started, follow recipe through to the end without stopping.

Heat oven to 350 degrees.
Place two salad plates and two salad forks in freezer to chill.

Fine dice two white onions and set aside. *(Fine dice is ⅛-inch cubes. See Tips and Techniques.)*

Chop ⅛ cup parsley and set aside.
Peel and slice carrots thin. Set aside.

In a skillet, melt half a cube butter over medium heat. Do not allow butter to burn. *(If butter burns, clean skillet and start over. Burnt butter will give the finished dish a burnt taste.)*

Place veal slices between wax paper, and pound with rolling pin or skillet to flatten and spread.

To the butter add half the white onion and sauté until tender. Add ¼ cup bread crumbs, ⅛ cup parsley, 1 teaspoon salt, and ⅛ teaspoon pepper. Mix well. Add ⅛ cup heavy cream and blend, then remove from heat.

In a second skillet, melt 1 tablespoon butter over medium heat.

Spread onion mixture on each veal steak.
Cut ham into 2-inch-wide strips and top the stuffing mixture with several ham slices. Roll up veal and tie each with string in two places.

Place veal rolls in butter and sauté on all sides until veal turns white. Place veal rolls in baking dish. Add the remaining diced onion, carrots, and ½ cup chicken stock. Cover with foil and place in oven.

Cut flowerets from broccoli.
Prepare vegetable steamer in pan with water. Add flowerets and cover, but do not turn on heat.

Place 2 cups chicken stock in pan for rice. Add 1 tablespoon butter. Do not turn on heat.

Wash spinach and tear leaves into bite-size pieces, and place in bowl. Discard stems.

Slice four rings from red onion, and set aside.
Add 2 tablespoons olive oil to spinach and toss to coat all spinach. Salt and pepper to taste and toss. Break onion rings apart and add to spinach. Add 1 tablespoon bacon bits.
Finely grate 2 tablespoons Parmesan cheese and add to spinach. Mix well and refrigerate.

Turn chicken stock to high heat.

In small pan, heat 1 tablespoon olive oil and 1 tablespoon butter over medium heat.
While oil heats, peel 2 cloves of garlic and thin slice. Add garlic to oil. Do not allow garlic to burn.
Add ½ teaspoon salt, ⅛ teaspoon pepper, and stir. Add juice from half a lemon, stir, and remove from heat.

Add 1 cup rice to boiling chicken stock and stir. Cover and reduce heat to low.
Set the table, set background music and take a 5-minute break with your guest.

Turn broccoli to medium-high heat. Quickly stir rice and cover.
Seat your guest, open the wine, and allow it to breathe.

Place salad on chilled plates, and serve with frozen forks.

When salad course is finished (about 10 to 15 minutes), clear plates.
Turn off broccoli, drain, and remove steamer from pan.
Return broccoli to pan and pour lemon garlic oil over broccoli, tossing to coat it.

Remove veal from oven. Do not discard cooking liquid.
Place two veal rolls on each ovenproof plate, and place plates in oven.
Mix 1 teaspoon cornstarch with 1 teaspoon hot water, and add to carrot-onion cooking liquid. Stir until sauce thickens. (If sauce does not thicken quickly, place over medium heat and continue to stir.)

Remove plates from oven. Place a bed of rice on each plate.
Place veal rolls on rice and spoon sauce over top. Garnish with chopped parsley top. Add broccoli to plate and serve.

Serves two.

To serve four, use 8 veal cutlets and 2 bunches broccoli. For the dressing, use ½ cup bread crumbs and ¼ cup cream. For the salad use 2 bunches spinach, 3 tablespoons oil, 8 onion slices, 2 tablespoons bacon bits, and 4 tablespoons Parmesan cheese. Follow the same directions.

# ⚜ Veal Bourguignonne on a Bed of Pasta

Boned veal chops browned in oil and simmered in beef stock and red wine with leeks, carrots, mushrooms, garlic, and sage. Served over egg noodles with corn blended with eggs, cream, and cheddar cheese, cooked until set. Recommended wine: Merlot.

---

**Total time: 60 minutes**

### Ingredients

2   large, thick veal chops
1   carrot
1   leek
2   cloves garlic
1   can beef stock
¾   cup red cooking wine
⅛   cup soy sauce
1   teaspoon sage
    Olive oil
3   tablespoons flour
1   tablespoon sugar
½   cup grated cheddar cheese
8   mushrooms
    Butter
1   can whole-kernel corn
    Salt and pepper
4   ounces egg noodles
2   eggs
⅛   cup heavy cream
1½  tablespoons cornstarch

### Utensils needed

Pot, large sauce pan with cover, medium sauce pan, skillet.

Once started, follow recipe through to the end without stopping.

Preheat oven to 250 degrees.

Bone the veal chops and cut into 1-inch-square chunks. Set aside. Peel carrot and cut into thin slices ⅛ inch thick. Set aside. (*Be sure all slices are the same thickness. This will allow all carrots to cook evenly.*)

Cut green end from leek, slice leek in half, and carefully wash out all sand between leaves. Slice leek thin and set aside. (*Leeks are grown in very sandy soil, so be sure all sand and grit is removed.*)

Peel 2 cloves garlic and crush with side of knife. Set aside. (*See Tips and Techniques for tips on peeling and crushing garlic.*)

In a large sauce pan, mix ¾ cup beef stock, ½ cup red cooking wine, 2 crushed cloves garlic, ⅛ cup soy sauce, and 1 teaspoon sage. Place over medium heat. Add leeks and stir.

In a skillet, heat 4 tablespoons olive oil over medium heat.

In a bowl, mix 3 tablespoons flour and 1 tablespoon sugar. Coat veal chunks in flour-sugar mixture. (*An easy way to coat veal is to put the flour-sugar in a zip-lock bag, add veal, and shake.*)

Sauté veal in oil until browned on all sides. Add veal to leek pan. Add carrots to veal, cover, and reduce heat to medium-low.

Grate ½ cup cheddar cheese, and set aside.
Cut stems from mushrooms and discard. Slice caps and set aside.

Place 1 quart water in pot for noodles, salt the water, and add 1 tablespoon oil. Do not turn on heat.

Drain corn. Place 1 tablespoon butter in pan, add corn, and place over medium heat.

Set the table.

Take a 10-minute break with your guest.

Stir veal. Add mushrooms to veal and add ½ teaspoon salt and ½ teaspoon pepper.
Turn pasta water to high.
Set background music, open the wine, and allow it to breathe.
Stir the corn.

When pasta water boils, add 4 ounces egg noodles and stir.
Place two ovenproof plates in oven to warm.

Seat your guest.
Stir the veal.

In a bowl, combine two eggs and ⅛ cup heavy cream, then beat with fork. Add egg-cream mixture to corn, mix well, and return to medium-low heat. Add ½ cup grated cheddar cheese to corn and mix to melt.

In a small glass, combine 1½ tablespoons cornstarch with 1½ tablespoons red cooking wine to form thick liquid. Add to the veal mixture and stir until sauce thickens. *(Mixture should thicken quickly. If not, increase heat, keep cooking, and stir for a few minutes, and it will thicken.)* Reduce heat to low.

Stir the corn.

When noodles are tender, drain them.
Remove plates from oven and place noodles on each plate. Top with veal and spoon sauce over top.
Add corn to plate and serve.

Serves two.

To serve four, use 4 large veal chops, 2 carrots, 2 leeks, 4 cloves garlic, 1½ cups beef stock, 1 cup red wine, ¼ cup soy sauce, 2 teaspoons sage, and 16 mushrooms. Follow the same directions.

# ✿ Veal Scaloppine in Mushroom Gravy on Rice

Thin veal scaloppine lightly browned and blended with sautéed onion, mushrooms, white wine, diced tomatoes, sherry, and mushroom gravy. Served over white rice with Brussels sprouts poached in bouillon, vermouth, and nutmeg, with a lemon butter. Recommended wine: Pinot Noir.

---

**Total time: 55 minutes**

## Ingredients

| | |
|---|---|
| ¼ | pound mushrooms |
| 1 | tomato |
| 1 | small white onion |
| 10 | to 12 Brussels sprouts |
| 1 | lemon |
| ¾ | pound veal scaloppine |
| | Wax paper |
| ½ | tablespoon dry vermouth |
| 1 | chicken bouillon cube |
| | Nutmeg |
| | Salt and pepper |
| | Butter |
| | Olive oil |
| | Flour |
| 1 | pouch Success Rice™ |
| | Dry white cooking wine |
| 1 | jar Heinz™ mushroom gravy |
| 2 | tablespoons sherry |
| | Fresh parsley |

## Utensils needed

Large skillet, pot, two sauce pans.

---

Once started, follow recipe through to the end without stopping.

Preheat oven to 250 degrees.

Cut stems from mushrooms and discard. Slice caps, and set aside. Large dice ½ cup tomato, and set aside. (*Dicing a tomato requires the same technique as for onions. Large dice is ½-inch cubes. See Tips and Techniques for dicing instructions.*)
Dice 1 tablespoon onion, and set aside.
Trim bottom end off Brussels sprouts, and set aside.
Finely grate ¼ teaspoon lemon rind, and set aside. (*Grate the yellow part only. The white flesh is bitter.*)

If veal is in steak form, slice into strips about 1 inch wide. Place veal strips between wax paper, and pound with rolling pin or heavy skillet to flatten and spread. (*Veal should be about ¼ inch thick.*)

Set the table.

Place 1 cup water in sauce pan and add ½ tablespoon vermouth, 1 bouillon cube, a dash of nutmeg, and ⅛ teaspoon pepper. Cover, and place over low heat.

In a second sauce pan, melt half a stick butter over medium-low heat.

Place 2 quarts water in pot for rice, salt the water, and place over medium-high heat.

In a skillet, heat 3 tablespoons olive oil over medium-high heat.
Season veal with salt and pepper, and dredge in flour.
Take a few minutes with your guest until oil is hot.
Sauté veal in butter until lightly browned on both sides (about 5 minutes).

While veal cooks, remove pan with melted butter from heat. Stir in ¼ teaspoon lemon rind and juice of half a lemon, and set aside.

When veal is browned on both sides, remove to plate.
Add sliced mushrooms to skillet and sauté until soft.

Turn water with bouillon to medium heat

Add 1 pouch Success Rice™ to boiling water in pot.

When mushrooms are soft, reduce heat to medium-low and add
¼ cup white cooking wine and 1 tablespoon diced onion. Sauté until
liquid is reduced by one-third. (*Reducing liquid will increase and
concentrate the flavors by the same proportion.*)

When mushroom liquid is reduced, add ½ cup chopped tomato and
1 cup Heinz™ brown mushroom gravy. Mix well. Add veal strips
and mix. Add 2 tablespoons sherry and mix.

Place Brussels sprouts in bouillon water, cover, and turn to high heat.

Take a 5-minute break with your guest.

Place two ovenproof plates in oven to warm. (*Warmed plates keep food
warm 30 percent longer than cold plates.*)

Set mood music, seat your guest, and open the wine.

Drain rice.
Open pouch and add rice to each plate, top with veal strips, and
spoon sauce over rice and veal.
Drain Brussels sprouts, add sprouts to lemon butter, and stir to coat.
Add sprouts to plate and spoon lemon butter over top.
Garnish plate with parsley and serve.

Serves two.

To serve four, double all
ingredients and follow
the same directions.

# 🌸 Veal Parmigiana on a Bed of Pasta

Veal cutlets, egg-dipped and breaded in Parmesan cheese and seasoned bread crumbs, then browned, baked in an Italian sauce, and topped with melted Swiss cheese. Served on a bed of spaghetti, with a sauté of garlic, onions, and celery. Recommended wine: Merlot.

---

**Total time: 50 minutes**

### Ingredients

1   bunch celery
1   onion
2   eggs
½   cup seasoned bread
    crumbs
½   cup Parmesan
    cheese
    Salt and pepper
2   cloves garlic
    Olive oil
    Butter
1   can Contadina™
    pizza sauce
5   ounces thin
    spaghetti
2   veal cutlets
    Sliced Swiss cheese
    Fresh parsley

### Utensils needed

Large skillet, medium skillet, pot for pasta, baking dish.

Once started, follow recipe through to the end without stopping.

Preheat oven to 350 degrees.
Peel off outer stalks of celery and discard. Slice 4 to 5 stalks ¼ inch thick. Set aside. (*Slice celery on a 45-degree angle. This will produce a larger slice for better plate coverage and is a more attractive presentation.*)

Medium dice half the onion and set aside. (*Medium dice is ¼-inch cubes. See Tips and Techniques for quick dicing techniques.*)

In a bowl, beat two eggs with fork and set aside.

Mix ½ cup seasoned bread crumbs with ½ cup Parmesan cheese, ½ teaspoon salt, and ¼ teaspoon pepper. Set aside.

Finely chop two cloves garlic, and set aside. (*To peel garlic easily, gently crush garlic clove with flat of knife blade until skin breaks. The garlic will now peel easily. To finely chop, crush peeled clove with side of knife, then chop. See Tips and Techniques.*)

Place 2 quarts water in pot for pasta. Salt the water and add 1 tablespoon olive oil to water, and turn to high heat. (*The olive oil helps to prevent the pasta from sticking together.*)

Set the table.

In a medium skillet, melt 4 tablespoons butter over medium-low heat.

In a large skillet, place 4 tablespoons olive oil and turn to medium heat. When oil is hot, dip veal in egg and coat with bread crumbs on all sides. Sauté veal in oil until browned on both sides. (*Be sure oil is hot by testing with end of veal. Veal should bubble around edge. If oil isn't hot, the veal will soak up the oil instead of cooking quickly.*)

Place veal in baking dish. Pour pizza sauce over veal and place in oven.

Place 5 ounces spaghetti in boiling water, and reduce heat to medium-high.

Add chopped garlic to butter in the medium skillet, and sauté a few minutes.
Add celery and onion to garlic butter and stir to coat. Increase heat to medium.

Open the wine and allow it to breathe. (*This process allows the flavors to "open up."*)
Take a 5-minute break with your guest.

Place several slices of Swiss cheese on top of pizza sauce over each veal cutlet and return to oven.
Stir celery.

Place two ovenproof plates in oven to warm. (*Warm plates keep food hot 30 percent longer, giving you more time to prepare and serve plates.*)

Set background music.
Seat your guest.

Drain pasta and rinse under very hot tap water, and drain again.
Place pasta on warmed plate, top with veal and spoon sauce around edges.
Add celery, garnish with sprig of parsley, and serve.

Serves two.

To serve four, use 8 stalks celery, 1 onion, 4 veal cutlets, and 10 ounces pasta. Follow the same directions.

# &  Breaded Veal Scaloppine with Olive Tomato Sauce

*Egg-dipped veal scaloppine, sautéed until lightly browned, topped with a green olive, tomato, onion, garlic, and wine sauce, with oregano and basil. Served with sautéed mushroom caps and buttered peas. Recommended wine: Gamay Beaujolais.*

---

**Total time: 50 minutes**

### Ingredients

- ½ pound small mushrooms
- 1 small white onion
- 18 large stuffed green olives
- 1 package frozen peas
- 2 eggs
- 4 tablespoons olive oil
- 2 cloves garlic
  Flour
- 1 12-ounce can tomato paste
  Dry white cooking wine
- 1 teaspoon oregano
- 1 teaspoon basil
  Salt and pepper
- ¾ pound veal scaloppine, sliced in strips

### Utensils needed

Three skillets, sauce pan with cover.

---

Once started, follow recipe through to the end without stopping.

Preheat oven to 200 degrees.
Set the table.

In one skillet, melt 3 tablespoons butter over low heat.
While butter melts, wash mushrooms, cut off stems, and discard.
Set caps aside.

Finely dice ⅓ cup onion, and set aside. *(Fine dice is ⅛-inch cubes. See Tips and Techniques for dicing instructions.)*

Slice 18 stuffed olives, and set aside. Reserve 1 tablespoon olive liquid.

In a bowl, beat two eggs with fork, and set aside.

In a second skillet, heat 2 tablespoons olive oil over medium heat.
Peel two cloves of garlic and mash with side of knife blade. *(See Tips and Techniques.)*
Add garlic to oil, add ⅓ cup onions, and cook 5 minutes. Do not allow garlic to burn.

While garlic cooks, place ½ cup flour in bowl, and set aside.

When onions are cooked, remove garlic and discard.
Add ¾ cup tomato paste and 1 cup white wine to onions, and stir until blended.
Add 1 teaspoon oregano and 1 teaspoon basil, and mix well. Salt and pepper to taste, and reduce heat to low.

Place mushrooms in skillet with melted butter, and stir to coat mushrooms on all sides.
Increase heat to medium-low, and stir occasionally.

Fill pan with ¼ cup water for peas and place over high heat.

In a third skillet, place 2 tablespoons olive oil and 2 tablespoons butter. Do not turn on heat. *(Adding the oil will allow the butter to take a higher temperature without burning.)*

To tomato mixture add sliced olives and 1 tablespoon juice from olives. Stir.

Place two ovenproof plates in oven to warm. *(Warming plates will keep the dinner hot 30 percent longer than cold plates.)*

Open the wine and allow it to breathe. *(This will intensify the flavors and allow the wine to mellow.)*

Turn oil and butter to medium heat.
Add peas to boiling water, cover, and cook.

Take a 5-minute break with your guest.

Salt and pepper veal.
Coat veal with flour on all sides. Dip veal in egg and sauté in oil.

While veal cooks, set background music, and seat your guest.

Remove peas from heat, add 2 tablespoons butter, salt and pepper to taste, and mix.
Turn tomato sauce to medium-low and stir.
Turn veal over and sauté the other side.

Remove plates from oven.
Place veal on plate, and spoon tomato sauce over veal.
Add peas and sautéed mushrooms to plate and serve.

Serves two.

To serve four, use 1 pound mushrooms, ⅓ cup onion, 1½ cups tomato paste, 2 cups white wine, 2 teaspoons oregano, 2 teaspoons basil, and 1½ pounds veal scaloppine. Follow the same directions.

# ✿ Veal Marsala with Fettuccine Alfredo

*Veal·steaks sautéed in butter with mushrooms, lemon juice, and Marsala, garnished with lemon slices and capers. Served with fettuccine blended with sour cream, cream cheese, wine, fresh-grated Parmesan cheese, and buttered peas. Recommended wine: Pinot Noir.*

---

| Total time: 55 minutes |
|---|

### Ingredients

| | |
|---|---|
| 8 | medium mushrooms |
| 1 | lemon |
| ⅛ | cup olive oil |
| | Butter |
| 1 | package frozen peas |
| | Fettuccine noodles |
| 3 | ounces Philadelphia™ cream cheese |
| 2 | veal steaks about ¼ inch thick |
| ½ | cup Marsala or sherry |
| 1 | cup sour cream |
| 1 | tablespoon white cooking wine |
| 2 | tablespoons finely grated fresh Parmesan cheese |
| | Salt and pepper |
| | Capers |

### Utensils needed

Large skillet, pot for pasta, two pans.

Once started, follow recipe through to the end without stopping.

Preheat oven to 250 degrees.

Wash mushrooms, cut off stems, and discard. Slice caps thin and set aside.
Cut lemon in half and slice four thin slices from center. Set aside. Reserve lemon.

Place 2 quarts water in pot for fettuccine, salt the water, and add 1 tablespoon olive oil. Turn to high heat.

In another pan, melt half a stick of butter over low heat.
Add 3 ounces cream cheese to butter in pan.

Set the table.

When water in pot boils, add enough fettuccine for two (about 8 ounces) and reduce heat to medium-high.

In a skillet, melt 2 tablespoons butter over medium heat. Do not allow butter to burn. (*Burnt butter will give the finished dish a burnt taste. If butter burns, clean the skillet and start over.*)

Add ⅛ cup olive oil to butter and let heat until a drop of water "dances" when dropped into skillet. Sauté veal in skillet for 2 minutes on each side.
Add sliced mushrooms and stir.

Stir cream cheese to melt and blend with butter.

Take a 5-minute break with your guest.

Fill pan with ¼ cup water for peas, cover, and place over high heat.

Turn veal over, add juice from half a lemon (1 tablespoon) and ½ cup Marsala or sherry.

Reduce heat to low and simmer.

Add peas to water in pan, cover, and cook.

Finely grate 2 tablespoons Parmesan cheese, and set aside.

Place two ovenproof plates in oven to warm.

To butter and cream cheese add 1 cup sour cream, 1 tablespoon white wine, and 1½ tablespoons grated Parmesan cheese. Mix well. Season with salt and pepper to taste.

Check veal and mix.
Open the wine and allow it to breathe.
Set background music and seat your guest.

Remove peas from heat. Add 1 tablespoon butter and mix.
Drain fettuccine and rinse under very hot tap water. Drain again.

Place fettuccine on warmed plates and top with Alfredo sauce.
Add veal to plate and spoon mushrooms over veal.
Garnish veal with lemon slices and sprinkle capers over lemon slices.
Stir peas, add to plate, and serve.

Serves two.

To serve four, use 6 ounces cream cheese, 12 ounces fettuccine, 4 veal steaks, 12 mushrooms, 2 tablespoons lemon juice, ¾ cup Marsala, 2 tablespoons Parmesan, 1½ cups sour cream, and 2 tablespoons white wine. Follow the same directions.

# Lamb Dinners

Pan-Broiled Lamb Chops with Leeks in Cream

Mixed Lamb English Grill with Carrot Fritters

Pan-Broiled Lamb Chops Stuffed with Sausage

Garlic-Fried Lamb with Mint Sauce

Lamb Fricassee in Cream Sauce on Fettuccine

# 🧿 Pan-Broiled Lamb Chops with Leeks in Cream

Thick lamb chops rubbed with garlic and pan-broiled. Served with poached leeks in a thick cream sauce, blended with tarragon, basil, and thyme, and peas with fresh mint leaves and sugar. Recommended wine: Pinot Noir.

---

**Total time: 55 minutes**

### Ingredients

2   cloves garlic
4   lamb rib chops, 1 inch thick
    Olive oil
    Salt and pepper
4   small to medium leeks
2   sprigs fresh mint
    Butter
1   package frozen peas
1   bay leaf
1   teaspoon sugar
1   teaspoon flour
1   cup whipping cream
½   teaspoon tarragon
½   teaspoon basil
½   teaspoon thyme

### Utensils needed

Skillet, three pans.

---

Once started, follow recipe through to the end without stopping.

Preheat oven to 250 degrees.

Peel and crush two cloves garlic. (*See Tips and Techniques for easy ways to peel and crush garlic.*)

Trim the outer skin from lamb chops. Rub lamb chops with olive oil and with crushed garlic. Set aside.

Trim root and green end from leeks. Slice leeks into ½-inch-thick slices. Rinse under cold water to remove any sand. Let stand in water. (*Leeks are grown in sandy soil and may have a lot of grit inside leaves. Be sure to rinse thoroughly, or sauce will have a gritty texture.*)

Fill one pan with 4 cups water for leeks. Salt the water and place over high heat.

Mince two sprigs of mint. (*See Tips and Techniques for chiffonade cut.*)

Set the table.

Add leeks to boiling, salted water.
Take a 15-minute break with your guest.

In a third pan, melt 1 tablespoon butter over medium heat.

Place skillet over medium-high heat and add 1 teaspoon olive oil. (Do not add lamb chops.)

Drain leeks.

Fill second pan with ¼ cup water for peas and place over high heat.

To melted butter whisk in 1 teaspoon flour to form a paste. (*This is called a* roux, *which is the thickening agent in many sauces.*) Add ½ cup cream and whisk until smooth. Add remaining cream and whisk until smooth. Reduce heat to low. (*This is the basis for a béchamel or white sauce.*)

Place lamb chops in hot skillet. Sear on one side several minutes, turn, and continue cooking.

Add peas to boiling water and cover.

Add leeks to cream sauce and stir.
Add ½ teaspoon tarragon, ½ teaspoon basil, and ½ teaspoon thyme. Salt and pepper to taste and mix well.

Place two ovenproof plates in oven to warm. *(Warmed plates keep food hot longer, which is why restaurants heat plates. Cold plates quickly extract the heat from food.)*

Turn lamb chops and continue cooking.

Seat your guests and open the wine. *(This will allow the wine to "breathe" and the flavors to intensify.)*

Add mint, bay leaf, and 1 teaspoon sugar to peas and reduce heat to low.

When lamb chops are just cooked through, remove plates from oven. *(To check lamb, insert knife into center and twist. Lamb should be cooked with no red in center.)*
Place two lamb chops on each plate.
Add creamed leeks, mint peas, and serve.

Serves two.

To serve four, use 8 chops and 6 leeks. For sauce, melt 1½ tablespoons butter, add 2 teaspoons flour, 1¾ cups cream, and add 1 teaspoon each of tarragon, basil, and thyme. Follow the same directions.

# 🕸 Mixed Lamb English Grill with Carrot Fritters

*Boned lamb chops, pan-fried with sausage, bacon, chicken liver, onions, and tomatoes. Served with shredded carrots blended with eggs, flour and milk, then fried to make fritters, and seasoned mashed potatoes with brown gravy. Recommended wine: Zinfandel.*

---

| Total time: 60 minutes |
| --- |

### Ingredients

2   potatoes
2   lamb chops
    (4, if small)
2   small sausage links
1   slice bacon
6   pearl onions
2   tomatoes
8   mushrooms
4   medium carrots
    Butter
2   cloves garlic
2   tablespoons flour
2   tablespoons milk
    Olive oil
1   egg
1   tablespoon sugar
    Salt and pepper
1   jar brown gravy
2   chicken livers
¼   cup cream
1   0.4-ounce packet ranch
    buttermilk salad
    dressing mix

### Utensils needed

Large skillet, medium skillet, medium pan, small pan.

Once started, follow recipe through to the end without stopping.

Preheat oven to 200 degrees.

Fill medium pan ¾ full of hot water and place over medium-high heat.
Peel potatoes and dice into ½-inch cubes. Add potatoes to water.

Bone lamb chops, and slice meat into 1-inch squares. Set aside.
Cut sausage into 1-inch-long pieces, and set aside.
Cut bacon into 1-inch pieces, and set aside.
Peel onions, and set aside.
Chop tomato into ½-inch pieces, and set aside.
Cut mushrooms in half, and set aside.
Peel carrots and finely grate 1½ cups. Set aside.

Set the table.

Peel and crush garlic. (*Crush garlic by placing flat side of knife blade on clove and applying pressure with palm of hand. See Tips and Techniques.*)

Place 2 tablespoons butter in large skillet, add garlic, and place over medium-high heat. (*Watch carefully. Do not allow butter to burn or the meal will have a burnt taste.*)

In a large bowl, whisk together 2 tablespoons flour, 2 tablespoons milk, 1 tablespoon olive oil, and 1 egg. Mix well to form batter.
Mix in 1½ cups grated carrots and 1 tablespoon sugar. Mix well to coat carrots.

To melted butter add bacon, onions, lamb, and sausage. Salt and pepper to taste, and mix well.

Place gravy in small pan and place over medium-low heat.
Drain potatoes, return to pan, and place in oven.

Stir meat. Add chicken livers and mushrooms, and continue to cook.
Take a 10-minute break with your guest.

Stir meat.
In a medium skillet, heat 1 cup olive oil over medium-high heat.

Mash potatoes with potato masher or mixer.
Add 2 tablespoons butter, ¼ cup cream, and ½ packet of ranch dressing.
Mix well and keep warm in oven.

Place two ovenproof plates in oven to warm.

Add tomatoes to meat and mix well.

When oil is hot, mix carrot mixture and drop 1 tablespoon of mixture into skillet. Repeat to make four fritters. Cook until set, turn, and cook until lightly brown. Drain onto paper towels.

Remove plates from oven.
Add lamb grill to plate, add mashed potatoes, and top with gravy.
Add carrot fritters and serve with wine.

Serves two.

To serve four, use three potatoes, four lamb chops, four sausage links, two bacon slices, three tomatoes, and sixteen mushrooms. Make eight carrot fritters (you should have just enough batter). Follow the same directions.

# Pan-Broiled Lamb Chops Stuffed with Sausage

Lamb chops stuffed with sausage and pan-broiled. Served with vermicelli pasta blended with Swiss cheese, egg, milk, and nutmeg, then baked, and with poached endive, onions, and peas, lightly buttered. Recommended wine: Merlot.

---

**Total time: 45 minutes**

### Ingredients

1½ cups broken vermicelli
    Butter
1 can peas
1 onion
1 endive
2 round bone lamb chops, ⅝ inch thick
1 package Jimmy Dean Sausage™
½ pound Swiss cheese
½ cup milk
1 egg
    Nutmeg

---

### Utensils needed

Skillet, two pans (one with cover), small baking dish.

---

Once started, follow recipe through to the end without stopping.

Preheat oven to 350 degrees.

In a pan, bring 4 cups salted water to boil over high heat.
Break vermicelli into 3-inch-long pieces to yield 1½ cups.

In a pan with cover, place 1½ cups water and 1 tablespoon butter over medium-low heat.
Drain peas, and set aside.

Cut half the onion into ¼-inch-thick slices. Set aside. *(Be sure all slices are the same thickness to assure proper cooking.)*

Cut across endive in ½-inch-thick slices.
Add onion and endive to buttered water, cover, and let cook.

Take a 5-minute break with your guest.

Add vermicelli to boiling water, and stir.

Remove round bone from lamb chops. Rub chops with olive oil, then salt and pepper the chops. Form a 1-inch ball of sausage and place in hole where the bone was removed. Flatten sausage until it is the same thickness as lamb chop. Set aside.

Set the table.

Grate 1 cup Swiss cheese.
Butter small baking dish, and set aside.
In a bowl, mix ½ cup milk with 1 egg. Set aside.

Drain vermicelli. Place vermicelli in baking dish. Add Swiss cheese and mix with fork. Pour milk-egg mixture over top. Sprinkle lightly with nutmeg and place in oven.

Heat skillet over medium-high heat.

Take a 5-minute break with your guest.

Add peas to endive and stir. Continue to cook uncovered.

Place lamb chops in hot skillet.

Open the wine and allow it to breathe. *(This will allow the wine flavors to enhance.)*
Turn lamb chops and continue cooking.

Place two ovenproof plates in oven to warm. *(Warm plates will keep the food hot 30 percent longer.)*

Take a 5-minute break with your guest.

Turn lamb and continue cooking.

Drain endive mixture and return to pan. Add 1 tablespoon butter, and lightly stir to melt.

Remove plates from oven.
Place lamb chops on each plate.
Add vermicelli cheese pudding and endive-pea mixture, and serve.

Serves two.

To serve four, use whole onion, two endives, and four lamb chops. Follow the same directions.

# Garlic-Fried Lamb with Mint Sauce

*Small lamb chops rubbed with garlic and oil, then pan fried, with a fresh mint, sugar, and vinegar sauce. Served with a thick, browned-onion soup, topped with fresh Parmesan cheese and poached cabbage mixed with Swiss cheese and nutmeg, then baked. Recommended wine: Cabernet Sauvignon.*

---

**Total time: 60 minutes**

---

### Ingredients

- 4   large garlic cloves
- 4   small lamb chops
  1 to 1½ inches
  thick
-     Olive oil
-     Salt and pepper
- ½   cup fresh mint, chopped
- 1   large white onion
- 1½  tablespoons sugar
- ½   cup vinegar
- 2   cups chicken stock
- 3½  tablespoons butter
- 1   small cabbage
- 8   ounces fresh grated Parmesan cheese
- 4   ounces Swiss cheese
- 1½  tablespoons flour
- ⅛   teaspoon nutmeg
- 1   teaspoon cornstarch

---

### Utensils needed

Small pan, two medium pans, pot, skillet, baking dish.

---

Once started, follow recipe through to the end without stopping.

Preheat oven to 350 degrees.

Peel garlic cloves and purée with side of knife. *(See Tips and Techniques for peeling and mashing garlic.)* Rub lamb chops with olive oil and crushed garlic. Salt and pepper the chops. Set aside.

Chop ½ cup fresh mint leaves, and set aside.
Boil 3 tablespoons water in small pan over high heat.

While water comes to boil, peel onion and slice into ¼-inch-thick slices and set aside.

Dissolve 1½ tablespoons sugar in boiling water.
Remove from heat and add ½ cup mint leaves and ½ cup vinegar. Mix and set aside.

Place 2 cups chicken stock in medium pan over high heat.

Melt 1½ tablespoons butter in skillet over medium-high heat. Do not allow butter to burn.

Cut half the cabbage into ½-inch chunks and set aside.

Add onion slices to butter, pushing rings apart. Increase heat to high fry until onions brown.

While onions fry, finely grate ½ cup Parmesan cheese, and set aside. Grate 1 cup Swiss cheese, and set aside.

Stir 1½ tablespoons flour into onions, and, while stirring, cook for 2 minutes.
Transfer onions to boiling chicken stock, reduce heat to medium-low, cover, and let cook. Save the skillet onions were cooked in.

Place 6 cups water in pot, place over high heat, and salt well.

Set the table, then take a 10-minute break with your guest.

Add cabbage to boiling water.
Remove onion soup from heat, stir, cover, and let stand.
Add 1 tablespoon butter to skillet the onions were fried in, and place over medium-high heat.

Butter a 7- x 9-inch baking dish, and set aside.

Seat your guest and open the wine.

Place lamb chops in skillet.
Place soup in bowls, top with grated Parmesan cheese, and serve the first course.

When soup course is finished (approximately 10 minutes), turn lamb chops and reduce heat to medium-low.

Drain cabbage and return to pot.
Add 1 tablespoon butter and mix to melt. Add grated Swiss cheese and ⅛ teaspoon nutmeg.
Mix and transfer to baking dish, then place in oven.

Place two ovenproof plates in oven to warm.
Place mint sauce over high heat.

Check lamb, and remove from heat if browned.

Mix 1 teaspoon cornstarch with ½ teaspoon water and add to mint sauce, stirring constantly until sauce thickens. Remove from heat.

Place two lamb chops on plate.
Spoon desired amount of mint sauce over lamb. Garnish with mint leaves.
Add cabbage-cheese bake and serve.

Serves two.

To serve four, use 4 lamb chops, ¾ cabbage, and 1½ cups grated Swiss cheese. For soup, use 2 onions, 4 cups chicken stock, and 3 tablespoons flour. Follow the same directions.

## 🦞 Lamb Fricassee in Cream Sauce on Fettuccine

Boned lamb sautéed in garlic butter, blended with béchamel sauce, and simmered with diced onions, thyme, and sage. Served over fettuccine pasta with a cassarole of layered braised lettuce, oregano, sliced tomatoes, mushrooms, and Fontina cheese. Recommended wine: Gamay Beaujolais.

---

| Total time: 55 minutes |
|---|

### Ingredients

|       | Butter |
|-------|--------|
| 1½    | pounds round bone lamb chops |
| 1½    | tablespoons flour |
| 1     | cup cream |
|       | White pepper |
| 1     | white medium onion |
| 2     | cloves garlic |
| 1     | teaspoon thyme |
| ½     | teaspoon sage |
| ½     | pound mushrooms |
| 2     | large tomatoes |
| 1     | iceberg lettuce |
| 1     | cup grated Fontina cheese |
| 1     | teaspoon oregano |
|       | Salt and pepper |
| 8     | ounces fettuccine |

### Utensils needed

Small pan, medium pan with cover, pot, baking dish.

Once started, follow recipe through to the end without stopping.

Preheat oven to 350 degrees.

Melt 1½ tablespoons butter in small pan over medium heat.
Trim and bone lamb, cut into ½-inch pieces, and set aside.
To butter add 1½ tablespoons flour, and mix to blend.
Add ½ cup cream and whisk until sauce smoothes and thickens.
Add remaining ½ cup cream, and whisk to blend and smooth sauce.
Add a pinch of salt and ⅛ teaspoon white pepper. Remove from heat and set aside.

Peel onion and dice small. (*Small dice is ⅛-inch cubes. See Tips and Techniques for easy way to dice onion.*)

Fill pot three-quarters full with hot tap water and salt. Place over high heat.

In a medium pan, melt 2 tablespoons butter over medium-high heat. Do not allow butter to burn.
Peel and crush two cloves garlic with side of knife and add to butter. (*See Tips and Techniques.*)
Add lamb to butter and sauté, stirring to coat lamb with butter. Cook until lamb turns color on all sides.
Reduce heat to low. Add diced onion, white sauce, 1 teaspoon thyme, and ½ teaspoon sage. Mix well, cover, and let cook.

Set the table.

Clean mushrooms, quarter, and set aside.

Cut a small X in smooth end of each tomato. Drop tomatoes into hot water for 20 seconds. Remove from water with spoon, and allow water to continue heating over high heat.
Peel tomatoes by pulling skin at points of X.

Core the lettuce and cut half into quarters. Add lettuce to boiling water.

Stir lamb.

Grate 1 cup Fontina cheese, and set aside.
Butter a 7- x 9-inch baking dish.
Slice tomatoes into ¼-inch-thick slices, and set aside.

Remove lettuce from water with spoon, and let drain. Keep water in pot and return to high heat. Add an additional 2 cups hot tap water to pot.

Peel lettuce leaves apart and line baking dish with leaves. *(Lettuce will be hot, so use a spoon to separate the leaves.)*
Place layer of sliced tomatoes over lettuce and sprinkle with 1 teaspoon oregano.
Add a layer of mushrooms, and salt and pepper to taste. Sprinkle half the cheese over mushrooms. Repeat this process with another layer of lettuce, tomatoes, mushrooms, and cheese. Place in oven.

Add 8 ounces fettuccine to boiling water and stir to separate pasta so it won't stick together.
Turn off heat under lamb and let stand, covered, on burner.

Take a 5-minute break with your guest.

Stir fettuccine.

Open the wine and allow it to breathe.
Place two ovenproof plates in oven to warm.
Stir lamb. If the sauce is too thick, thin it with a little cream.

When pasta is done, drain and rinse under very hot water. *(To test pasta, pull one noodle out of water and bite into it. The noodle should be soft, with slight resistance. This is* al dente, *which means "to the tooth.")*

Remove plates from oven.
Place a bed of pasta on each plate. Top with lamb and sauce.
Add lettuce-mushroom-tomato bake and serve.

Serves two.

To serve four, use 2½ pounds lamb and 12 ounces fettuccine. Follow the same directions.

# Brunches

Crab and Asparagus with Monterey Cheese Sauce
on an English Muffin

Eggs Benedict with Fresh Fruit

Quiche Lorraine with Wilted Spinach Salad

Clam Chowder with Corn Fritters

Scallop, Cheddar, and Onion Omelet with
Sour Cream and Chives

# 🦀 Crab and Asparagus with Monterey Cheese Sauce on an English Muffin

Toasted, buttered English muffin, topped with blanched asparagus spears, fresh crab meat, and a Monterey Jack cheese-cream sauce. Served with a tomato, green onion, and butter lettuce salad with a basil garlic dressing. Recommended wine: Blanc de Blanc.

---

**Total time: 40 minutes**

### Ingredients

| | |
|---|---|
| | Olive oil |
| | Red wine vinegar |
| 2 | cloves garlic |
| 2 | teaspoons basil |
| | Salt and pepper |
| 1 | bunch fresh asparagus |
| 1 | block Monterey Jack cheese |
| 1 | large tomato |
| 1 | bunch green onions |
| 1 | head butter lettuce |
| | Butter |
| ½ | pound crab meat (fresh) |
| ½ | cup heavy whipping cream |
| 1 | English muffin |

### Utensils needed

Skillet, two small pans, bowl.

---

Once started, follow recipe through to the end without stopping.

Place two wine glasses in freezer to chill.
Set the table. (Fresh flowers add a nice touch to the table.)

In a bowl, combine ¼ cup olive oil, 2 teaspoons wine vinegar, 2 cloves peeled and crushed garlic, and 2 teaspoons basil. *(To crush garlic, place flat side of knife blade on clove and apply pressure with heel of hand. See Tips and Techniques.)*
Salt and pepper to taste, mix well, and set aside.

Clean asparagus and cut tops into 4-inch-long spears.
Grate ¾ cup Monterey Jack cheese and set aside.

Thin slice tomato.
Thin slice green onion.
Place full leaf of lettuce on each of two small plates. Arrange tomato slices on lettuce, sprinkle with green onion, and place in refrigerator.

Heat 1 quart water in pan over high heat.

Melt 1 tablespoon butter in skillet over low heat.

Check crab meat for any shell pieces and add to butter.

In another pan, place ¼ cup whipping cream and turn to medium heat.

When water boils, add asparagus and boil 4 minutes.

Add cheese to cream and stir to melt cheese.
Split English muffin and place in oven under broiler to toast.

While asparagus cooks, seat your guest and serve the wine. *(Don't forget the chilled glasses.)*

Stir cheese mixture until melted and smooth.

Drain asparagus.

Butter English muffin. Place muffin on each plate, and add four to five spears of asparagus on top.
Layer with crab and spoon cheese sauce over top.

Spoon dressing over salad and serve.

Serves two.

To serve four, double all ingredients except lettuce. Follow the same directions.

# 🌸 Eggs Benedict with Fresh Fruit

Toasted English muffin with ham slice, topped with a poached egg and hollandaise sauce. Served with fresh strawberries, grapes, and melon. Recommended wine: Champagne.

**Total time: 35 minutes**

### Ingredients

    Cantaloupe
6   strawberries
1   English muffin
2   ham or Canadian
    bacon slices
    Butter
2   eggs
1   can Aunt Penny's
    Hollandaise Sauce™
    Worcestershire
    sauce
    Grapes
    Fresh parsley
    Coffee

### Utensils needed

Egg poacher, small pan, skillet.

First, make coffee and serve to your guest. (*If Sunday, a nice touch is the Sunday paper served with coffee.*)

Once started, follow recipe through to the end without stopping.

Place two champagne glasses in freezer to chill.

Turn oven to 250 degrees.

Cut cantaloupe into wedges and place in refrigerator.
Clean strawberries, cut off stem end, and set aside.
Cut English muffin in half and butter both halves.
Cut two slices of ham or Canadian bacon ⅛ inch thick, and set aside.

Prepare egg poacher with water and place on high heat. Add dab of butter to each poacher.
(*If you don't have an egg poacher, you can poach eggs in water with 1 tablespoon vinegar. With a spoon, swirl boiling water in pan and slide egg into water. The vinegar will hold the egg together. When done, remove with slotted spoon.*)

Place ham slices in skillet over medium heat.
Place English muffins in oven.

Place hollandaise sauce in small pan, and add two to three shakes of Worcestershire sauce. Mix well over low heat. Stir occasionally.

Arrange cantaloupe wedges, strawberries, and grapes in two small bowls and return to refrigerator.

When egg water boils, turn ham slices. Place eggs in buttered poaching cups, place in poacher, cover, and poach 4 minutes.

While eggs poach, place two ovenproof plates in oven to warm.

Set the table, and set background music. (*A fresh flower arrangement on the table adds a festive touch.*)

Just before eggs are poached, place English muffin on warmed plate. Top with slice of ham.

Turn out poached egg on ham, and spoon hollandaise sauce over egg.

Sprinkle pepper over top, and garnish with parsley.

Serve eggs benedict and fruit bowl.

Open champagne and enjoy. *(Don't forget the chilled glasses. See the wine section in the Introduction for the proper way to open champagne.)*

Follow brunch with coffee, if desired.

Serves two.

To serve four, double all ingredients and poach four eggs. Follow the same directions.

## ⚙ Quiche Lorraine with Wilted Spinach Salad

A quiche with a bread crust and layers of onion, Swiss cheese, bacon, and shallots, topped with an egg-and-milk mixture, sprinkled with nutmeg, and baked. Served with a warm, wilted spinach salad, with a hint of vinegar. Recommended wine: Champagne.

---

**Total time: 50 minutes**

### Ingredients

1   pound bacon
1   onion
1   bunch green onions
2   shallots
¾   pound block Swiss cheese
    Fresh strawberries, grapes, and melon (enough for two)
4   eggs
1   cup Half & Half™
1   tablespoon Bisquick™
    Butter
1   box seasoned croutons
    Nutmeg
2   bunches spinach
2   tablespoons vinegar

### Utensils needed

Skillet, small baking dish, pot.

---

Once started, follow recipe through to the end without stopping.

Preheat oven to 375 degrees.
Place two champagne glasses in freezer to chill.
Place two small bowls in freezer for fruit.
Set the table.

Cook bacon in skillet until crispy. (*An easy way to cook bacon is to spread bacon on cookie sheet and place in oven at 400 degrees. Turn when top starts getting crispy, and drain off grease. Continue cooking.*)

While bacon cooks, thin slice onion, and set aside.
Chop green end of green onion, and set aside.
Dice shallot, and set aside.
Slice swiss cheese ⅛ inch thick, and set aside.

Clean strawberries, cut off stem end, and cut strawberries in half.
Clean grapes.
Cut half the melon into wedges and cut off rind. Cut melon wedges into bite-size pieces.
Mix all fruit in bowl and refrigerate.

Drain bacon on paper towel and save bacon grease. Dice bacon with knife, and set aside.

Place eggs in bowl and beat with fork. Add 1 cup Half & Half™, 1 tablespoon Bisquick™, and diced shallots. Blend with fork or whisk.

Butter a small (7- x 9-inch) baking dish. Cover bottom with single layer of croutons.
Separate onion rings, and cover croutons with thin layer.
Sprinkle with one-third of the bacon, sprinkle green onions over bacon, and cover with a single layer Swiss cheese. Repeat layer of onions, one-third of the bacon, green onions, and cheese. Save the last third of bacon for salad.

Pour egg mixture over quiche until it just covers top.
Sprinkle top with nutmeg and place in oven.

Bake until egg mixture is set in center, about 35 minutes.

While quiche bakes, clean spinach leaves and cut off stems. *(Spinach is grown in sandy soil, and you may taste a gritty texture if leaves are not thoroughly washed.)*

Place spinach leaves in large bowl, and set aside.

Take a break with your guest until quiche is almost done.

In a skillet, heat 3 tablespoons bacon grease over medium heat. Add 2 tablespoons vinegar, the last third of diced bacon, and ⅛ teaspoon pepper. Mix well.

Place two ovenproof plates in oven to warm.
Seat your guest.

Place fruit in frozen bowls and serve.

Remove quiche from oven and cut into pie-shaped pieces. Place on warmed plate.

Pour hot bacon oil over spinach leaves and toss, coating all leaves. Serve.
Open champagne. *(Don't forget the chilled glasses. See wine section in the Introduction for tips on the proper way to open champagne.)*

Serves two.

To serve four, increase fruit to yield four servings. Follow same directions. You should have enough quiche and salad to serve four.

# ☙ Clam Chowder with Corn Fritters

*A rich clam chowder with potatoes, bacon, onion, celery, shallots, and basil, simmered in cream with baby clams. Served with creamed corn blended with flour, sugar, and eggs, then fried into fritters. Recommended wine: Grey Riesling.*

| |
|---|
| **Total time: 55 minutes** |

## Ingredients

- 1   potato
- ¼   pound bacon
  Olive oil
- 1   onion
- 1   stalk celery
- 1   shallot
- ½   teaspoon beau monde (found in spice section)
- ½   teaspoon pepper
- ½   cup grated cheddar cheese
- 3   eggs
- 1   tablespoon sugar
- ½   cup creamed corn
- ½   cup whole-kernel corn
- ½   cup flour
- 1½  teaspoons baking powder
- ⅛   cup Half & Half™
  Salt
  Butter
- 1   10-ounce can whole baby clams
- ½   teaspoon basil
- 1½  cups heavy cream

## Utensils needed

Two-quart pot, two sauce pans, skillet.

Once started, follow recipe through to the end without stopping.

Place two wine glasses in freezer to chill.
Set the table.

Peel potato and cut into quarters. Fill sauce pan three-quarters full of water, add potato, and place over high heat.

Cut ¼ pound bacon into ½-inch-square pieces.
In a pot, heat ½ tablespoon oil over medium-high heat. Add bacon to oil and sauté.

Medium dice half the onion, and add to bacon. (*Medium dice is ¼-inch cubes. See Tips and Techniques for quick, easy way to dice onion.*)

Chop ¼ cup celery, and add to bacon.
Finely chop shallot, and add to bacon.
Add ½ teaspoon beau monde and ½ teaspoon pepper, and sauté until browned. Stir often, and do not allow to burn.

Heat oven to 250 degrees.
Grate ½ cup cheddar cheese, and set aside.

In a bowl, beat or whisk three eggs.
Add ¼ teaspoon salt and 1 tablespoon sugar, then blend.
Add ½ cup creamed corn, ½ cup whole-kernel corn, ½ cup flour, ½ tablespoon baking powder, ⅛ cup Half & Half™, and grated cheddar cheese. Mix well, and set aside.

Add 1 cup oil to skillet. Do not turn on heat.

Remove potato from heat and drain.

When bacon mixture is sautéed, remove and save sautéed ingredients.
In the same pot over medium heat, melt a quarter stick butter.
Drain clams, but save the juice. Add clams to butter. Add ½ teaspoon basil and mix.

Dice potato into small chunks, and add to clams.
Add sautéed ingredients to clams.
Add clam juice and 1½ cups cream and mix.

Turn oil in skillet to medium heat.
Take a 5-minute break with your guest.

Stir chowder.

When oil is hot, drop 1 heaping tablespoon of fritter batter into oil, 1 inch apart. *(Oil will be hot enough when a drop of water "dances" in skillet. If oil is not hot enough, the fritters will soak up the oil and have an oily taste.)*
Fry until browned on bottom, turn, and brown other side.
Remove fritters and drain on paper towels. Place fritters on plate and place in oven.
Repeat with remaining fritter batter, making four fritters.

Set background music and seat your guest.

Ladle chowder into bowls, place bowls on large plate, and place two fritters on each plate. Serve.
Open the wine and enjoy. *(Don't forget the chilled glasses.)*

Serves two.

To serve four, make eight fritters. You should have enough batter to do this. The chowder should also serve four without increasing any ingredients.

# 🌸 Scallop, Cheddar, and Onion Omelet with Sour Cream and Chives

Whisked eggs blended with Tabasco and cream, cooked with chopped scallops, onion, and cheddar cheese, folded over and topped with sour cream and fresh chives. Served with a garlic butter sauté of portabello, oyster, and button mushrooms. Recommended wine: Champagne.

---

| |
|---|
| **Total time: 45 minutes** |

### Ingredients

 1  onion
 4  eggs
 ¼  cup cream
    Tabasco
 ½  teaspoon tarragon
 10 to 12 small scallops
 4  ounces cheddar
    cheese
    Fresh chives
 1  portabello
    mushroom
 1  handful oyster
    mushrooms
 8  common mushrooms
 1  clove garlic
 1  tablespoon butter
 2  tablespoons olive oil
 1  8-ounce sour cream

### Utensils needed

Two 10-inch skillets, one with cover.

Once started, follow recipe through to the end without stopping.

Preheat oven to 200 degrees.

Place two champagne glasses in freezer to chill.

Fine dice ¼ cup onion, and set aside. *(See Tips and Techniques for instruction on fine dicing.)*

In a bowl, whisk eggs, 4 shakes of Tabasco, and ¼ cup cream until frothy. *(The introduction of air into the eggs will make the omelet fluffy and light.)*
Add ½ teaspoon tarragon and mix well.

Course chop scallops, and set aside.
Chop chives, and set aside.
Grate ½ cup cheddar cheese.

Wash mushrooms. Slice portabello cap into ⅛-inch-thick slices, chop stem, and set aside.
Quarter common mushrooms, and set aside.

Peel and crush 1 clove of garlic. *(See Tips and Techniques for easy ways to peel and crush garlic.)*

In the first skillet, melt 1 tablespoon butter over medium-low heat.

Set the table. Set background music.

Pour egg mixture into skillet, with melted butter. Sprinkle diced onion over eggs.
Sprinkle chopped scallops over half of the eggs.
Cover and let cook.

In a second skillet, heat 2 tablespoons olive oil and crushed garlic over medium heat.

Add all mushrooms to hot garlic oil and toss to coat mushrooms. Place two ovenproof plates in oven to warm.

Take a 5-minute break with your guest, or make coffee at this time.

Sprinkle ½ cup cheddar cheese over same half of eggs as scallops. Cover and continue to cook.

When eggs are set in center, loosen edges with spatula, and fold plain side over scallop-cheese side. Let stand off the heat.

Toss mushrooms.
Remove plates from oven.
Lightly salt omelet and cut it in half with spatula. Place omelets on plate, top each with a dollop of sour cream, and sprinkle with chopped chives.
Add mushrooms to plate and serve.

Open champagne and serve in chilled glasses. *(See wine section in the Introduction for proper technique for opening champagne.)*

Serves two.

To serve four, double all ingredients, and make two skillets of omelet.

# Desserts

Baked Almond Custard Pie

Ginger Snap Baskets Filled with Fresh Fruit or Ice Cream

Warm Whiskey Sauce over Ice Cream or Pound Cake

Lemon Sherbet with Frozen Vodka and Raspberries

Vanilla Peach Pudding Cake

Crepes Suzette

Country Cherry Cobbler

# Baked Almond Custard Pie

### Ingredients

¼  cup firmly packed brown sugar
¾  cup slivered almonds
1  can sweetened condensed milk
5  eggs
1  cup whipping cream
1  teaspoon almond extract

Preheat oven to 325 degrees.
Place slivered almonds on baking sheet and toast in oven. (*This will bring the oil in the almonds to the surface for a richer flavor.*)

Sprinkle brown sugar on the bottom of an 8-inch-round, nonstick cake pan, and set aside.

Grind toasted almonds in food processor.
In a bowl, whisk together ground nuts, 1 can sweetened condensed milk, 5 eggs, ½ cup cream, and 1 teaspoon almond extract. Blend thoroughly.

Pour into cake pan.
Set cake pan in larger pan holding 1 inch of hot water. (*This will prevent the custard from burning on the bottom.*)
Bake 45 minutes or until knife inserted in center comes out clean. (*The ground almonds will rise and form a crust on the top.*)

Let cool, and then chill in refrigerator.

To serve, beat ½ cup whipping cream until stiff.
Run knife around edge of pie and invert onto serving plate.
Garnish with whipped cream and slivered almonds. (*Piping the whipped cream on top with a pastry bag makes a professional presentation.*)

Serves eight to ten.

# Ginger Snap Baskets Filled with Fresh Fruit or Ice Cream

### Ingredients

¼  cup butter
½  cup superfine sugar
1  teaspoon ground ginger
⅓  cup light corn syrup
½  cup flour
   Parchment kitchen paper

Preheat oven to 350 degrees.
In a sauce pan, over medium-low heat, combine ¼ cup butter, ½ cup sugar, 1 teaspoon ginger, and ⅓ cup light corn syrup. Heat until butter melts. Stir, remove from heat, and let cool.

Blend in ½ cup flour and incorporate well.

Line baking sheet with parchment paper. Drop heaping teaspoonful of dough onto baking sheet, allowing 5 to 6 inches between each. (*You will only get three on a baking sheet. They will spread to about a 6-inch circle when baked.*)

Bake 10 minutes or until edges begin to darken.

Remove from oven and let cool a few seconds. (*They will be full of bubbles.*)
Turn upside down on work surface and peel off parchment paper. Working quickly, pick up cookie and mold over upside-down coffee cup or small bowl, pulling edges to flute. Let harden, then remove cup mold. (*If cookie hardens before you can form it, return to oven for a few seconds and it will soften.*)

For serving, fill with ice cream or fresh fruit and top with whipped cream.

Yields six to eight baskets.

# Warm Whiskey Sauce

## Ingredients

½  cup butter
1 ½  cups powdered sugar
1  egg yolk
½  cup bourbon

Cream butter and sugar over medium heat until all butter is absorbed. Remove from heat.

Blend in 1 egg yolk.
Gradually add bourbon, stirring constantly. (*Add bourbon to taste.*)

Sauce will thicken as it cools.

To serve, heat sauce over medium-low heat until warm. Spoon warm sauce over ice cream, pound cake, or bread pudding.

Serves six.

# Lemon Sherbet with Frozen Vodka and Raspberries

## Ingredients

6  ounces vodka
   Lemon sherbet or lemon ice cream
   Raspberries

Freeze vodka for 3 hours. (*Vodka will not freeze, but it will thicken.*)
Place six champagne glasses in freezer to chill.

Place lemon sherbet in six chilled champagne glasses.
Pour 1 ounce frozen vodka over each glass.

Sprinkle a few raspberries in each glass.

# Vanilla Peach Pudding Cake

## Ingredients

3  tablespoons butter
¾  cup flour
1  package vanilla instant pudding mix
1  teaspoon baking powder
1  egg
½  cup milk
1  16-ounce can sliced peaches
1  8-ounce cream cheese, at room temperature
½  cup sugar
1  tablespoon sugar
½  teaspoon cinnamon

Preheat oven to 350 degrees.
Melt butter over low heat. Do not allow butter to burn.

In a bowl, mix flour, vanilla pudding mix, and 1 teaspoon baking powder.

In a second bowl, combine 1 egg, ½ cup milk, and melted butter. Add to dry ingredients and mix well to form batter.

Butter a 7- x 9-inch baking dish.
Spread batter evenly in bottom of baking dish.

Drain peaches, and reserve ⅓ cup peach juice. Chop peaches and sprinkle evenly over batter.

In a bowl, beat cream cheese, adding ½ cup sugar, a little at a time, until blended. Add ⅓ cup peach juice, and beat until blended. Spread over chopped peaches.

Combine 1 tablespoon sugar with ½ teaspoon cinnamon and sprinkle over cream cheese mixture.

Bake 45 to 50 minutes, let cool, and serve.

Serves six to eight.

(*Can be served cold or reheated 15 minutes at 250 degrees and served warm.*)

# Crepes Suzette

## Ingredients - Crepe batter

2  eggs
¾  cup milk
⅔  cup beer
1  cup flour
¼  teaspoon salt
2  tablespoons olive oil

In a bowl, beat or whisk all ingredients until smooth. Set aside to thicken, about 15 minutes.

Brush a 10-inch nonstick skillet with oil and place over medium heat until a drop of water "dances."

Pour 2 ounces (¼ cup) in center of skillet and quickly roll skillet to spread batter over bottom.
Cook a few minutes until edges start to brown. Turn crepe and cook a few seconds longer.

Makes seven to ten crepes.

*(Crepes can be made ahead and frozen between sheets of wax paper. To thaw, let stand at room temperature for 5 minutes.)*

## Ingredients - Crepes Suzette

4  crepes
1  lemon
1  orange
3  tablespoons butter
   Vanilla extract
1  teaspoon sugar
½  cup Curaçao
½  cup brandy

Finely grate 1 teaspoon lemon rind. *(Yellow part only. The white has no lemon oil and tends to be bitter.)*

Finely grate 1 teaspoon orange rind. Juice the orange and set juice aside.

Melt 3 tablespoons butter in skillet over medium heat.
Add lemon and orange rind, the juice from 1 orange, a few drops of lemon juice, a few drops of vanilla extract, 1 teaspoon sugar, and ½ cup Curaçao. Heat to boil.

Fold crepes into quarters. Place crepes in sauce, spooning sauce over crepes. Heat to boil.

Pour ½ cup brandy into skillet and carefully ignite at side.
Serve immediately, while flame is still present.

Serves four.

# Country Cherry Cobbler

## Ingredients

½  cup butter (1 stick)
¾  cup sugar
2  eggs
½  teaspoon almond extract
1  cup flour
1  teaspoon baking powder
1  can cherry pie filling

Preheat oven to 350 degrees.

In a large bowl, beat butter and sugar until blended.
Add ½ teaspoon almond extract and 2 eggs. Mix until blended.
Beat in ½ cup flour and blend until smooth.
Add ½ cup flour and 1 teaspoon baking powder and blend until mixed well. This will make a thick batter.

Butter a 7- x 9-inch baking dish. Smooth batter evenly over bottom.
Spoon cherry pie filling in spots evenly on top, using about three-quarters of the can.

Bake at 350 degrees for 45 minutes or until toothpick inserted into cake section comes out clean.

Serves six to eight.

# Napkin Folding

## Crown

Iron and spray starch napkin on both sides.
Fold napkins before starting to prepare dinner.

Fold in half.

Fold left and right points to top point.

Fold bottom point to 1 inch below top point.

Fold point back to bottom edge.

Pinch at bottom and turn over.
Fold sides back and tuck together.

Turn down peaks and tuck in.

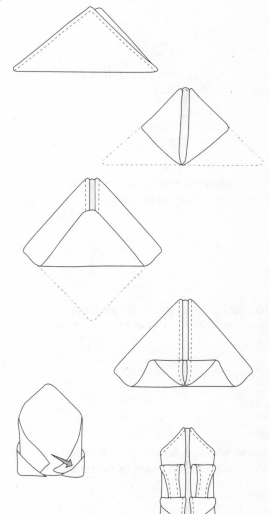

# Blossom

Iron and spray starch napkin on both sides.
Fold napkins before starting to prepare dinner.

Fold each corner to the center.

Repeat same procedure, folding each
corner to the center.

Carefully turn napkin over and once again
fold each corner to the center.

Keeping fingers on, reach under each corner
and gently pull out point to form peaks.

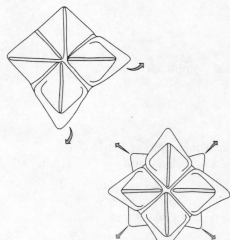

Now, reach under the center of each
side and pull out point of material.

# Elegant

Iron and spray starch napkin on both sides.
Fold napkins before starting to prepare dinner.

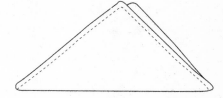

Fold napkin in half.

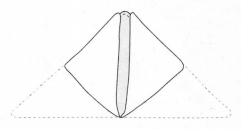

Fold each corner to top point.

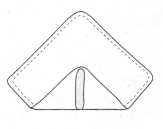

Carefully turn napkin over
and fold bottom corner up about 2 inches.

Fold sides underneath on a slight
diagonal and press lightly to set folds.

# Diagonal

Iron and spray starch napkin on both sides.
Fold napkins before starting to prepare dinner.

Fold napkin in half.

Fold in half again.

Roll down top flap.
Tuck second flap behind roll.
Tuck third flap behind second flap,
making three even strips as shown.

Carefully fold back the sides.

For informal dining, the silverware can be
placed in the pocket formed by strips, or a fresh
flower can be inserted into the folds.

# Tower

Iron and spray starch both sides of napkin.
Fold napkins before starting to prepare dinner.

Fold napkin in half, point to point.

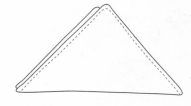

Fold edge up 1 inch.

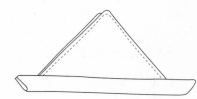

Carefully turn over and roll, tucking tip A
into rolled fold B.

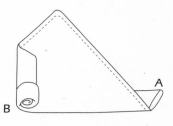

Stand on table or plate.

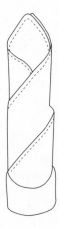

# Wave

Iron and spray starch napkin on both sides. Fold napkins before starting to prepare dinner.

Fold napkin into thirds.

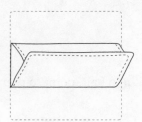

Fold each end over about 2 inches.

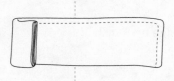

Fold both ends to meet in center.

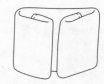

Fold sides back at center where ends meet.

Lay on table and carefully slide sections to make three even sections.

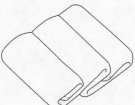

# Pocket

Iron and spray starch napkin on both sides.
Fold napkins before starting to prepare dinner.

Fold napkin into quarters with loose edges at
the lower right.

Fold first flap up to top point.

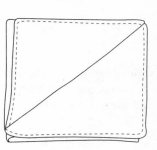

Fold second point up to 1 inch from first point.
Repeat with third and fourth points.

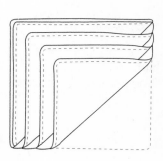

Place hand on top and carefully fold sides back.

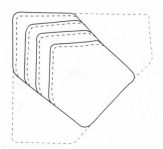

For picnics and informal dining, the silverware
can be slid between the first and second flaps.

# Fan

Iron and spray starch napkin on both sides.
Fold napkins before starting to prepare dinner.

Fold napkin in half vertically.

Fold bottom edge up 1 inch, then back and forth
to form 1-inch accordion pleats.
Stop 4 inches from top edge.

Fold in half.
Rotate 90 degrees, holding accordion fold.

Fold tip of loose corner behind first pleat.
Stand on plate and let go.
Sides will fall, forming fan.

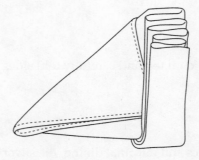

# Gourmet Roll

Iron and spray starch napkin on both sides.
Fold napkins before starting to prepare dinner.

Fold corner points to center.

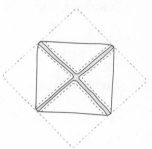

Fold in half horizontally.

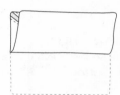

Fold right half over left.

Roll first flap down.

Tuck second flap under first.

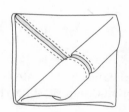 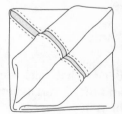

Carefully fold sides underneath.

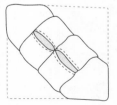

# Sailboat

Iron and spray starch napkin on both sides.
Fold napkins before starting to prepare dinner.

Fold in half, point to point.

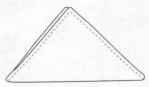

Fold left half over right.
Turn triangle so loose edge faces you
as noted by "bottom."

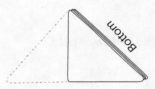

Fold bottom up 1 inch, twice.

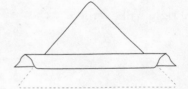

Bend in half backwards, stand up on plate,
and tuck left flap around and into right flap to
hold in place.

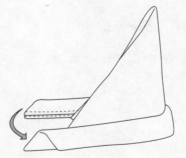

# Index

Vanilla Peach Pudding Cake, 131
Veal
   Breaded Veal Scaloppine with Olive Tomato
      Sauce, 100–101
   Stuffed Veal Rolls with Vegetable Sauce, 92–93
   Veal Bourguignonne on a Bed of Pasta, 94–95
   Veal Chops Baked in Sour Cream and
      Mushrooms, 90–91
   Veal Chops Cordon Bleu, 88–89
   Veal Marsala with Fettuccine Alfredo, 102–103
   Veal Parmigiana on a Bed of Pasta, 98–99
   Veal Scaloppine in Mushroom Gravy on Rice,
      96–97
Vegetable sauce, 92–93
Vegetables
   artichoke hearts, marinated, 24–25
   asparagus, baked, 62–63
   asparagus, steamed, 25–26, 38–39
   asparagus spears, blanched, 118–119
   broccoli, 92–93
   broccoli, steamed, 22–23, 40–41
   Brussels sprouts, poached, 96–97
   cabbage, 88–89, 90–91
   cabbage, poached, 112–113
   cabbage, sautéed, 12
   carrots, 72–72, 78–79, 94–95, 108–109
   carrots, sautéed, 16–17
   cauliflower, fried, 70–71
   cauliflower, steamed, 22–23, 26–27
   celery, 78–79, 98–99
   celery, sautéed, 52–53
   celery root, 82–83
   corn, 74–75
   corn, sautéed, 58–59
   cucumber, sautéed, 54–55
   endive, poached, 110–111
   escarole, 62–63
   green peas, 76–77
   green peppers, 84–85
   green pepper, sautéed with thyme, 24–25
   leeks, 72–73, 94–95
   mushroom caps, sautéed, 100–101
   mushrooms, 72–73, 94–95, 102–103
   mushrooms, garnish, 16–17
   mushrooms, gravy, 96–97
   mushrooms, sautéed with thyme, 24–25
   mushrooms, simmered in cream sauce, 38–39
   mushrooms, sliced, 30–31
   onion, poached salmon and, 48–49
   onions, 72–73, 78–79, 84–85

onion soup, 112–113
onions, sautéed, 12–14, 52–53, 96–99
onions, simmered in cream sauce, 38–39
peas, 30–31, 106–107
peas, buttered, 102–103, 110–111
peas, green, 76–77
peas, sautéed, 100–101
peppers, green, 84–85
peppers, sautéed, 46–47
potato slices, browned in oil, 14–15
potatoes, 72–73, 108–109
potatoes, baked, 56
potatoes, diced, 58–59
spinach, blanched, 16–17
spinach, creamed, 50–51
spinach, sautéed, 58–59
spinach, wilted, 56–57
squash, summer, steamed, 66–67
squash, yellow, sautéed, 54–55
sugar peas, steamed, 28–29
summer squash, steamed, 66–67
tomato-onion salad, 20–21
tomatoes, 82–83, 84–85, 96–97
tomatoes, sautéed, 12–14, 58–59
tomatoes, sliced, 48–49
tomatoes, stewed, 12
yams, 76–77
yellow squash, sautéed, 54–55
zucchini, sautéed, 12–14, 20–21
zucchini, stewed, 66–67
*see also* Preparation techniques
Vermicelli
   with beef Wellington, 68–69
   with pan-broiled lamb chops, 110–113
Vinegar and oil dressing, 44–45
Vinegar and sugar sauce, 112–113
Vinegar, mustard, and chive dressing,
   70–71


Warm Whiskey Sauce over Ice Cream or Pound
   Cake, 131
White rice, 18–19, 48–49, 82–83, 96–97
White wine, 3
White wine cream sauce, 38–39
Wild rice, 42–43, 54–55
Wine, 3–5
   in cream sauce, 38–39
   red, 3–4
   white, 3

Wine-Poached Salmon with Béarnaise Sauce, 48–49

Yams, 76–77
Yellow squash, sautéed, 54–55

Zucchini
sautéed, 12–14, 20–21
stewed, 66–67